A GRINGA IN BOGOTÁ

"June Erlick's deep understanding of Colombia has allowed her to write this engaging and enlightening personal narrative about the country's long-lasting, ongoing, but often forgotten civil war."

—JOHN WOMACK JR., R. W. BLISS PROFESSOR OF LATIN-AMERICAN HISTORY AND ECONOMICS, HARVARD

"The vignettes June Carolyn Erlick presents are a mirror image of everyday life from all corners of Bogotano society. Her achievement is possible due to her discipline in bringing back her deeply embedded memories of Bogotá and weaving them with her new experiences in 2005–2006. The city changes, the city remains. Thin, flea-infested dogs have gone for good but only apparently. Pit bull terriers and the like are nowadays a central piece of democratic security. *Desplazados* no longer find a place to squat like fifty years ago. Bogotanos are now proud of belonging. Superbus Transmilenio is the ensign of civic culture and modernity."

—MARCO PALACIOS, RESEARCH PROFESSOR AT EL COLEGIO DE MÉXICO AND FORMER RECTOR, NATIONAL UNIVERSITY, BOGOTÁ

"June Carolyn Erlick is a *gringa* in Bogotá who returns after thirty years to live in a city that never let her leave. In her book, she achieves what few manage: to write about Colombia without mentioning presidents, beauty queens, or drug lords. She also never talks about the war. However, the war permeates every page of the book, just as it permeates the lives of all of us Colombians."

—JUANITA LEÓN, AUTHOR OF *COUNTRY OF BULLETS* (2009) AND 2006 HARVARD NIEMAN FELLOW

"This is not a book about customs and manners, nor is it a tourist guide, nor a denunciation, nor a resounding investigation; it is a book that mixes all of these elements in the memories and impressions of a brilliant *gringa* who loves Colombia."

—DANIEL SAMPER PIZANO, AUTHOR AND COLUMNIST FOR *EL TIEMPO*, BOGOTÁ, COLOMBIA; 1981 HARVARD NIEMAN FELLOW; 1982 RECIPIENT OF MARIA MOORS CABOT PRIZE

"This testimony about the changes in Bogotá and about the relationship of one person—the author—with the city is fascinating and precise. The text asks time and again: How has the flowering of Bogotá incorporated in a subtle and nuanced manner the imprinted violence that has besieged so many parts of the country? How in the historical context of so much pain are so many moments of forgetting and happiness possible?"

—ANTANAS MOCKUS, FORMER BOGOTÁ MAYOR.

A Gringa in Bogotá

Living Colombia's Invisible War

BY JUNE CAROLYN ERLICK

University of Texas Press ◂◦▸ *Austin*

Originally published in Spanish by Aguilar, October 2007.

Cover illustration by Juana Medina.

Copyright © 2010 by June Carolyn Erlick
All rights reserved
Printed in the United States of America
First edition, 2010

Requests for permission to reproduce material from this work
should be sent to:
    Permissions
    University of Texas Press
    P.O. Box 7819
    Austin, TX 78713-7819
    www.utexas.edu/utpress/about/bpermission.html

⊗The paper used in this book meets the minimum requirements
of ANSI/NISO Z39.48-1992 (R1997) (Permanence of Paper).

LIBRARY OF CONGRESS CATALOGING-IN-PUBLICATION DATA

Erlick, June Carolyn.
    A gringa in Bogotá : living Colombia's invisible war / by June
Carolyn Erlick. — 1st ed.
        p.   cm.
    ISBN 978-0-292-72135-7 (cl. : alk. paper) — ISBN 978-0-292-
72297-2 (pbk. : alk. paper)
    1. Erlick, June Carolyn—Travel—Colombia—Bogotá. 2. Bo-
gotá (Colombia)—Description and travel. 3. Bogotá (Colombia)—
Social conditions. 4. Americans—Colombia—Bogotá. I. Title.
    F2291.B64E75   2010
    986.1'48—dc22   2009044435

For Micaela and Sara Luna,
Santiago and Sebastián,
and Manuela,
the future of Colombia and the planet

Contents

Can a city be in love with itself?

To wonder whether this can be, whether a city can be in love with itself, is not like asking whether people love their city. For that is a rather banal question. Of course they do. That is, many, many citizens feel strongly about their city. They know it, its streets, parks, stores, stadiums, theatres. Their homes. Many grew up there and have memories, long and short. They know their life through their city. They fall in love and marry, have children, bury their parents, go dancing. They know the smells of the city.

To say that people love their city is not to say that they do so all the time, or that their love is unconditional. It cannot be, not for a person, and not for a place. They can get angry and exasperated at their city and at their experiences there. Their love can ebb. They can be angered, even feel betrayed by their city, yet another sign that they are so deeply attached to it. Some can be indifferent, of course, and if so, they do not love it. But what is so striking is how very rarely we run into people who are indifferent to their surroundings, to the spaces in which they live. People attach themselves to spaces.

That the citizens of Bogotá are forever expressing their deep affection and their pride in their city to June Carolyn Erlick should thus not come to us as a surprise. But it does of course, especially to those who have not been there, and perhaps all the more so to those living in the United States. The State Department tells Americans that they should not travel there, for the city and the country are too dangerous. I cannot organize a study-abroad program there for students at the University of Virginia. Even if the government and the university were to allow it, I am sure that many of my students' parents would object. And understandably so. The newspapers here in the United States tell of homicides and bombs and crime and cocaine and paramilitaries and guerrillas and wars there. And they are right. All that is there. And Bogotá is in a poor country, so its citizens are almost certainly mainly poor. Bogotá is a city with a great deal of poverty. We know that without ever having been there.

Virtually all the titles of books published in the United States that seek to reveal what daily life is like in Colombia express tales of doom and destruction: *The Saddest Country*; *More Terrible Than Death*; *Walking Ghosts*; *Counting the Dead*; *Evil Hour in Colombia*; *The Dispossessed*; *A Genocidal Democracy*; *My Colombian War: A Journey through the Country I Left Behind*; *Colombia: A Brutal History; Law in a Lawless Land*. And there is the book by former senator and presidential candidate Ingrid Betancourt, *Until Death Do Us Part: My Struggle to Reclaim Colombia*. Betancourt, also a French citizen, was held captive in the jungles of Colombia for six long years, until she and fourteen others were rescued in a spectacular military mission on July 2, 2008. Her melancholy face broadcast to the nation, together with her searing letter to her family published in the last days of 2007, had brought the cruel realities of kidnapping to all Colombians and to many others throughout the world. Her book was a best seller in France when it appeared in bookstores there, and she now spends her time campaigning for peace. Her book, as all of these works, speaks to critically important realities in Colombia. They are also blinkered looks. These texts make me wonder what it would be like if I introduced Colombians to contemporary life in the United States with Dickensian texts like *In Search of Respect: Selling Cocaine in the Barrio* and with *Random Family: Love, Drugs, Trouble, and Coming of Age in the Bronx* and *American Ruins* and *The New American Ghetto*. *American Pictures: A Personal Journey through the American Underclass*, a pictorial and textual history by a Danish photographer is the most traumatizing book I have ever held in my hands.

Occasionally a title published in the United States will reflect something a bit different, as, for example, *Inside Colombia: Drugs, Democracy and War*. Some less immediate works, texts of history, do as well, as does *Between Legitimacy and Violence: A History of Colombia, 1875-2002*, and *Colombia: A Nation in Spite of Itself*. Still others, in English, are *Democracy in Colombia: Clientelist Politics and Guerrilla Warfare*, and *The Politics of Coalition Rule in Colombia*. So too do we have a book by a French historical sociologist that has not been translated into English. Its title is *Order and Violence*. And there is another recent book that is not in English: *La Nación Soñada: Violencia, Liberalismo y Democracia en Colombia*, written by a Colombian historian who keeps insisting that his nation is not such a bad place at all. And on Bogotá itself, there has just appeared *Gorgeous Monster: The Arts of Governing and Managing Violence in Contemporary Bogotá*. The city is a monster, to be sure, but a gorgeous one. There is violence, but it appears that it is being managed, at least to some degree. And governing in Colombia can be seen as an art.

Perhaps the works I have penned, one a historical monograph and another a memoir, *The Assassination of Gaitán: Public Life and Urban Violence in Colombia* and *Our Guerrillas, Our Sidewalks: A Journey through the Violence of Colombia*, might fit somewhat in this latter category of texts. There is an assassination and urban violence, but also a public life. There is violence in the title, but guerrillas and sidewalks are strangely tied. While one is largely about a riot and the other about a kidnapping, in both I am centrally concerned with *convivencia*, the abiding historical desire to live together in harmony that Colombians keep holding on to. *Convivencia* is a subject that permeates the pages of June Erlick's *A Gringa in Bogotá*.

As I walk the streets of this city today looking for clues, trying to get a feel for it, watching its citizens walking to and fro, checking up on those sidewalks, I keep wondering about that assassination that took place in 1948. My mother has always said that I would turn out to be a bit strange, a historian, because of the horrible fright she suffered that afternoon. On the way downtown for her appointment with the gynecologist, she just managed to climb into a cab and get away as the crazed crowds were streaming in her direction. My father calmly ordered that the hardware store he was managing be quickly locked up when he heard the rumor that Gaitán, the most popular political leader in the nation's history—but not someone he thought well of— had been killed just a few blocks away. He told his employees to make it back to their homes as soon as they possibly could, and he too started walking until he reached his house, five or six miles away.

Those crowds destroyed Bogotá in a few hours as no city of the Americas has ever been destroyed. I can't possibly imagine such a riot ever happening again, anywhere in Latin America or in the United States. The next morning, and for months to come, *bogotanos* could think only of London and Hamburg and Dresden, destroyed by bombs, as they looked aghast at what was left of their city. Few could imagine that the rage, the feeling of revenge, the sense of despair in Gaitán's mass followers could wreak such devastation.

That riot came to be known in Bogotá and throughout Colombia as *el 9 de abril*, the ninth of April, the date on which it erupted. In the rest of the world it became the Bogotazo. Has that afternoon percolated in the consciousness of *bogotanos*, leading them somehow over these years to treasure peace and understanding with an intensity that they might not otherwise have felt? I don't know. It's possible.

After *el 9 de abril*, the rural violence that had begun earlier, pitting followers of the Liberal and Conservative parties against one another, intensified horribly and would continue on for at least another ten years. By then, the lives of more than 170,000 Colombians had come to a violent end. During all those years, rural people streamed out of the countryside into the cities, and to Bogotá, seeking to save their lives, searching for peace, for some semblance of security. They left that rural past behind. We call this period La Violencia, with a capital *V* to distinguish it from all the other periods of violence in the nation's history, before and since. Did these displaced people, these frightened and forlorn internal immigrants, these impoverished peasants now without land or resources, come to yearn for a sense of togetherness, for that civility that now is so much of what Bogotá is about? Did they help bring it about? I don't know. It's possible.

What I do know over all these sixty years, and this may well be a form of evidence about what riot and violence have brought to the city, is that old *bogotanos* and new have hushed about those pasts. They have not wanted to talk about them, to remember them. *Bogotanos* have been thinking of the future, one that will be better for many of them. They have set about refashioning their individual and their collective lives.

When I was in Bogotá in 1988 negotiating for the release of my American brother-in-law, who was being held in captivity by the guerrillas who have been active out there in the countryside since the years of La Violencia of the 1950s, I kept running into fellow *bogotanos*, friends and strangers alike, who were moving forward with their lives while I was stuck trying to solve a human predicament that had started days, weeks, and months before. To me, the contrast between their lives and mine was jarring. Their outpouring of emotion at our travails moved me deeply. Their ability to distance themselves from my reality, and often also from their own public predicaments, struck me all the more. Over and over they said, "Don't worry. This will all end well." Over and again they talked and talked about themselves, about their nation and their history. They were not violent, they said. Colombia was a nation of hardworking people. *Bogotanos* talked about work. It is as though I had finally found the Protestant work ethic, and in a Catholic country. This was a people on the move. Some of those realities were those that I tried to capture in that memoir, a book that I have come to call, not the kidnapping book, but the sidewalks book.

The city I briefly lived in then, almost twenty years ago, was not yet the city that June Carolyn Erlick joins in 2005. But it was almost certainly on its way there. Back then it was at some kind of midpoint between the dark, sad, staid, colorless, and often rude place that I grew up in during the 1950s and '60s, and the city that is revealed to us in these pages. And when I return now to marvel at all that strikes my eyes and my senses, I am not there yet either, for I am caught somewhere between the past and the present.

Last summer I went downtown to join a massive demonstration against the guerrillas and the kidnappings. Once I was in the crowd, my body tightened up, and I looked with suspicion on all those around me, with surging anger at them as I was bumped about. That is the way I used to be as a kid in the city. We were that way in Bogotá, cursing easily at one another, lashing out, being disdainful of those below us on the social ladder. Slowly it began to dawn on me that I was not a stone in their river, that I kept getting in the way of others. The people around me who did not know one another, who had never been together before, were cooperating with one another, making room for the elderly, for mothers with children, sharing a space they had come to join. They were all breathing more deeply than I was. I kept trying to keep my spot, as though it were mine. I didn't see children being passed from person to person to allow them to get a better view, or to help their parents move about more easily, as Erlick does, but I am sure this was only because I was not at the right place, or because I left too early. And soon all those around me were noticing how knotted up I was. But they didn't say anything to me. Once I was in my home again, I felt grateful that they had not.

On rereading June Carolyn Erlick's pages about this city filled with polite soldiers, that is, with many soldiers and police officers, male and now female too, who treat the citizens of the city with politeness, I remembered how on arriving at that demonstration I glowered at a cop who was trying to quickly pat me down just to check, perfunctorily, for any weapons that I might be carrying. I blurted out some aggressive words at him, something about how my rights were being violated. I don't remember exactly what I said. He looked at me in surprise, his eyes wide open, as did many others around us too, as though I were a body from Mars. The city has changed. Bogotá is no longer the city I once knew.

It seems that in this city today even the most basic, individual act, even just walking from one place to another, becomes a collective experience. *El Tiempo*, the nation's major newspaper, runs a blog called *La ciudad jamás contada* (www.eltiempo.com/blogs/la_ciudad_jamas_contada/), where citizens are invited to write their histories in the city, their experiences, thoughts, and reflections. How fitting that people are now being asked to tell publicly about their lives in Bogotá. Soon, from *la ciudad jamás contada*, the city never told about, it will turn into *la ciudad más contada*, the city most told about. Here is Adriana Garcés, age thirty-three, an architect:

Camino por la calle y veo rostros que expresan todo tipo de emociones, cada uno tiene su propia historia y me imagino cuántos están viviendo la misma historia personal, cuántos comparten los mismos sufrimientos, las mismas emociones, y cuántos tienen las soluciones a los problemas de los demás en sus manos, es posible que yo misma. Sean el ángel guardián de alguien más, es posible que yo pueda aliviar ese dolor que otro sufre, es posible que yo pueda compartir esa dicha que a otro desborda, pero ¿por qué no nos damos cuenta de que en nosotros mismos está la respuesta a esa pregunta que todos tenemos en el alma?

[I walk the streets and I see all the faces expressing every emotion, each one has its own history, and then I wonder how many of us are living the same personal history, how many share the same sufferings, the same emotions, and how many have the same solutions right at hand to each other's problems. I might even have them. Even if they are someone else's guardian angel, it might just be that I could smooth the pain they suffer. I might be able to share in the happiness that overcomes another person. But why is it that we do not realize that the answer to the question that we all have in our souls is within each of us?]

Erlick discovered a city different from the one I encountered in 1988. I wasn't looking for it, living deep in my own troubles, and truth be told, this city was just beginning to emerge. The city I saw was a city at work. I was waiting, sitting around, endlessly expecting the guerrillas to call, all the while walking the sidewalks of the city, with nothing else to do. Around me others were being productive.

Travelers know they will come and go. Erlick goes to see

whether she might stay, to decide whether this is a place where she might retire a few years hence. She is an outsider who wants to be inside. Travelers ask whether this is a place where others can live. Erlick records a city she thinks about for herself. Is this where I want to live the last years of my life? Is this my place? Can I make it my own? Can I belong? She writes less and less as an outsider without ever becoming an insider.

Erlick's city is a city at play. Bogotá is a city on display. In this urban space people hurl themselves onto the street. This verb is the key word of this historical and contemporary lived experience in Bogotá. This is the collective impulse that is captured in these pages. Hurl. To hurl. When we use the word, we usually think of an object sailing through the air, a projectile we have flung away from us. In the experience of *bogotanos*, their bodies are hurling. People hurl themselves. At the same time, they are not acting alone, so that the hurling is also more than they, something that impels them. It is a collective impulse. There seems to be something pushing people in the back, propelling them forward into the street. Thus, they hurl themselves and are hurled.

Erlick gets the word from the Spanish word *arrojar*. *Se arrojan*. They hurl themselves. In Spanish too we can more easily think of *arrojar* as referring to something being thrown, rather than ourselves. Erlick quotes a journalist who writes that "during 14 days tens of thousands of citizens hurl themselves [*se arrojan*] into the streets to respond to a collective act of participation in an immense celebration of the imagination." *Bogotanos* are participating in the yearly theatre festival that is taking place, with drama performed in theatres, on streets, in parks, in schools, in workplaces, seemingly everywhere.

I have joined crowds before, and felt all the better for it, somehow empowered, liberated, beyond myself. But I suspect that this Bogotá hurling is somehow different, and more than what I have experienced. *Bogotanos* are not just becoming part of a crowd, and not just part of the city. Once hurled, they are the city. They are performing Bogotá and all that it means to them.

Bogotanos appear to be forming into something akin to what

Elias Canetti in his *Crowds and Power* calls feast crowds. Erlick's readers will recognize them.

> For the individual the atmosphere is one of loosening, not discharge. There is no common identical goal which people have to attain together. The feast *is* the goal, and they are there. The density is very great, but the equality is in large part an equality simply of indulgence and pleasure. People move to and fro, not in one direction only. . . . By common enjoyment at this one feast people prepare the way for many future feasts. . . . The feasts call to one another; the density of things and people promises increase of life itself.

Cannetti's feast crowd is agricultural in origin, celebrating food and abundance. In Bogotá the feast *is* the crowd itself, and there are reasons for this indulgence. It is urban and urbane, civil and polite. It is the city itself as its citizens want it to be. It is the city on display. It is peace performed, *convivencia* lived.

The closest symbol of this crowd is the river. "A river," writes Canetti, "is the crowd in its vanity, the crowd exhibiting itself. This being seen is as important as the element of direction. . . . They have a provisional goal, but it is not really important. The important thing is the stretch which separates them from it, the length of street they have to traverse. . . . Hence the fact that their origins are sometimes taken more seriously than their goal." In Bogotá it is the origins that count. Hurling. Origins mean that *bogotanos* can come together, can be together, can exist together. The goal is the crowd itself. The crowd is *convivencia*. At one moment sixty years ago the city was a reversal crowd bent on destroying everything. Now feast crowds day in and day out perform a collective exuberance.

Erlick chronicles the change that I have not lived, from that hierarchical, exclusive, disdainful, and even rude political culture of my youth to a softer, more convivial, more inclusive, more egalitarian civility of today. Erlick perceives these changes taking place in all walks of life in the city, and perhaps nowhere more simply than in language, from the use of the formal *usted*, with which I am still more comfortable, to the informal, more personal, more intimate *tú* as the forms of address that bring strangers together. So too with these crowds, conglomerations of people collectively engaged in a wide variety of public and personal pursuits. They are processions, but, far from the carefully organized ones from above from before, with the dignitaries of old at the start, they begin where they begin, in the tributaries, on side streets, daily, spontaneously. They begin by thousands of individual acts of hurling. These feast crowds have a whiff of democracy to them, a coming together with a sense of possible equalities that may well be more easily constructed and felt in public than they are in our daily private lives. The feast crowds express our better selves.

We write a lot these days about something called civil society. Often it is an abstract term, one with more theory in it than practice. Erlick's Bogotá is the detailed performance of just what might be meant by this civil society. We should not need to remind ourselves that civil society exists in a lived experience, in gestures. This is a book filled with such gestures, seen here and there, individually, on a bus, on a street, among strangers, between a soldier and a citizen.

And the wars out there in the countryside? What about that cocaine-infested violence, and the death squads, and the paramilitaries, and the massacres of impoverished rural people that have been such a central part of the nation's history since the 1980s? Do they not exist? Is this book too, from something like another side, yet another blinkered look at daily life in this city and in this country?

It is not. Erlick thinks continuously about those violent expressions of daily existence outside of Bogotá, in the countryside, in Colombia. More than that, Colombians in Bogotá are continuously telling her about that violence, about how it has affected them, their family, their friends, their society. *Bogotanos* don't let her forget about those violences that she cannot see in the city, but to which many of them are more personally connected than is she, as an outsider. And Colombians have come to Bogotá because of that violence, hurled from the countryside, unwillingly. As happened back in the 1950s, they arrive as refugees, as displaced people, *desplazados*, country folk, people who do not belong, people who by sleeping on doorsteps tell *bogotanos* that they too live in Colombia. More often than we wish to admit publicly, once they are there, we treat these newcomers like scum, like those inferior provincials who do not belong in the city among us. This too is Erlick's Bogotá. The *desplazados* are not part of our feast crowds. They are hardly even its spectators.

Would the citizens of Bogotá that Erlick tells us about feel impelled to launch themselves onto the street, into conviviality, were they not surrounded by all kinds of violent behaviors? If the events of 1948 and of the 1950s may well be working themselves out in the civic culture of the city today, those of the 1980s to our very day must certainly be making themselves felt on the way in which *bogotanos* go about their lives. Would they feel that little shove on their backs if much that surrounded them was just fine and dandy? To be sure, through their behavior *bogotanos* are expressing a long urban tradition that begins at least with Spanish colonial power, a tradition through which people distinguish themselves from the countryside and from country folk. For the citizens of this city, that need is all the deeper, for theirs is a nation with Latin America's longest-running armed conflicts. I am quite certain that the violence occurring in the countryside impels *bogotanos* to demonstrate to themselves and to others that they are not of that violence. The conflicts in the distance shove them into the streets. They are conscious of this need, of this desire, and they are not. They tell us in these pages that they are constructing a new society of solidarity and understanding, and they also tell us that they are simply acting, getting together, joining one another, living the city.

Erlick is between my past and this present. She chronicles the change, the transformation of the city. This is a rare vision of a place, of a city. Travelers more often just come and go. They offer us one passing glance, however deep. Erlick went long ago, fell for the place, and has been returning ever since. Now she has gone back for a year. Now she starts jotting down notes. The city won't let her just pass through. The city won't let her go. It is because it won't, because Bogotá is now Bogotá, that we have these pages. She wants to stay. She wants others, her readers, to know why. She writes.

Herbert Tico Braun
UNIVERSITY OF VIRGINIA

Preface

As a Fulbright scholar, a journalism professor, and a middle-aged, middle-class woman from the United States, I spent a year recently experiencing Bogotá. I wanted to figure out what it would be like to retire in the mountaintop city, and to understand how the often-invisible war is felt and experienced in this culturally vibrant metropolis. The war in the city is invisible, but constantly present in subtle ways, almost like the constant mist that used to drip down from the Bogotá skies so many years ago.

Perhaps I should have written "reexperiencing" rather than "experiencing," since I lived ten years in Colombia's capital city a generation ago as a foreign correspondent. It is a place where I experience the passage of time more intimately than at Harvard, where I am surrounded every year by students. In Bogotá, my life is woven into the lives of venerable friends older than me and of toddlers who call me Tía June—Aunt June.

In middle age, one looks back to not-so-distant youth and ahead to the joys and fears of old age. And I experienced the city in the same way, a city in the middle, facing the challenges of the war and the opportunities of the future. I found a city that had been transformed in a positive way, and yet I found myself constantly asking the question of how this change could coexist with an ongoing war. At first, I started thinking of Bogotá as an island, which it is indeed in a way, an oasis of urbanity and culture.

I started to write these vignettes in this book as a way of analyzing for myself the way the city—and I—had changed. I soon found that I was writing a peculiar kind of history—at once personal and collective.

I soon discovered that Bogotá is not an island; war and peace, civility and violence, together inhabit its streets. The war is at the door—invisible, present, and somehow integrated into daily life even when it appears absent. The war creates pressures on

Bogotá's urban infrastructure, as the number of displaced people and ex-combatants escalates.

The question is whether the new Bogotá with its culture of civic pride and urban civility can become a model for Colombia, whether the country as a whole can absorb these values, as well as create the necessary infrastructure and democratic participatory institutions that Bogotá has slowly begun to put in place. The alternative is that the pressures of conflict and even postconflict overwhelm the city, overwhelming its noble efforts and sweeping its notable gains away with the chaos of war and devastating inequality.

This book spans a highly specific time frame, 2005–2006. But at the same time, it reaches back and it reaches forward. It reaches back to my first period in Bogotá, but it also goes further back into a time before my own personal memory, a time of memory of my friends and my friends' parents and grandparents. Just as my childhood and frugal nature were influenced by the Great Depression, an event I never experienced but my mother lived as a young adult, the lives of Colombians are shaped by things that went before. And it reaches forward not only to my own future but also to the future of a city and a country that are part of me.

I am one of those who has lived in a foreign city that I feel has become my own. Whether or not I retire to my beloved city, my quest is an emotional, as well as an intellectual, one. It is one, I have found, that is shared, not only by Colombians in and beyond Colombia, by foreigners who study Colombia or who are married to Colombians or are otherwise in love with the city and country, but also by the growing diaspora of sons and daughters of Colombians abroad.

We share a love and a hope—and a future.

June Carolyn Erlick
CAMBRIDGE, MASSACHUSETTS
DECEMBER 2008

Acknowledgments

This book is the product of thirty-three years of journeys to Colombia, including the two periods I lived there, my *primera ronda*—the first time around—from 1975 to 1984 and on a Fulbright Fellowship in 2005–2006.

During all those years, many people have accompanied me in all sorts of ways. I need to thank all the Colombians, those who live there and those who live in the diaspora. I can't thank all the individuals, the taxi drivers and the tavern keepers, the journalists and the jurists, the waiters and the writers who have been my interlocutors over time.

I've been very lucky to have support from several institutions, including the Inter American Press Association, which awarded me a scholarship in 1977, allowing me to stay on in Colombia and begin my career as a foreign correspondent. The Fulbright Commission allowed me to return to Colombia for a year in 2005; I'd like to extend my gratitude to director Ann Mason, as well as Carol Robles in Washington, D.C., and to Peter Samson, then of the U.S. Embassy in Bogotá. The Harvard-MIT Club in Bogotá was generous and hospitable; the Columbia University Graduate School of Journalism, my alma mater, continued to provide me with inspiration and contacts. I especially want to thank the David Rockefeller Center for Latin American Studies at Harvard University and its then director John H. Coatsworth, now dean of Columbia's School of International and Public Affairs, for granting me the sabbatical and actually allowing me to enjoy it. I also appreciate the ongoing encouragement and generosity of Merilee S. Grindle, the present director, who has allowed me to flourish both as an editor and an author.

The Harvard-MIT Colombian Colloquium—founded in 1997, the same year I arrived at Harvard, after the conference "Law and Democracy in Colombia"—connected my life institutionally with Colombia and deserves an organizational thanks, as well as individual recognition of Liliana Obregón and Francisco Ortega; Enrique Chaux and Angelika Rettberg; César Abadía and Maria Russo; María Clemencia Ramírez and Andy Klatt; Rodrigo Villar, Claudia Uribe, and Manuela Villar; Claudia Pineda; María Piedad Velasco; and Antonio Copete, Diana Valencia, and so many others who made me feel not like a gringa in Bogotá, but like a *rolita*—a person from Bogotá—in Cambridge.

Colombia has provided me with deep and countless friendships, but at the same time these friends have become my interpreters in a complex world of contradictions and nuances. The family of Germán, Celia, Mauricio, and Adriana Rincón have been particularly notable in this sense. Their house in Bogotá has become my second home, with many Scrabble games mixed with conversations about politics and society over the years. I want to express a tender thank-you to them and to Inés Bolívar v. de Rincón, who died in March 2007, but not before teaching me a lot about Bogotá and life itself. May she rest in peace.

This book would not have been possible, and my life in Colombia would have been quite different, without the many people who helped me make sense of my daily experience. Just a few of these special people are Javier Moncayo; David Roll; Horacio Godoy; Leonel Narvaez; Roberto Gutiérrez; Eduardo Wills; Sara Giraldo; Ernesto Borda; Jorge Ramírez; Angela Pérez Mejía; Luis Ricardo Paredes Mansfield; Peter Montes; Carmen Millán de Benavides; Jorge Mario Múnera and Adriana Henao; Jack Womack; Theodore MacDonald; Héctor Rosero; Liza Higuera; Camila de Gamboa; Gloria Guardia; Sara de Mojica; Constanza Toquica; Marco Palacios; Consuelo Valdivieso; Azriel Bibliowicz and Doris Salcedo; and, above all, the Colombian journalists who have helped me and have accompanied me, who have taught me so much, especially Enrique Santos Calderón, Daniel Samper, Pilar Lozano, Leopoldo Villar-Borda, Mauricio Lloreda, Lorenzo Morales, Juanita León, and Margarita Martínez. I do not have the words to express to them how much I appreciate their help, support, and friendship. I also wish to thank Pilar Reyes and Tatiana Grosch, my editors of the book in Spanish.

Endless conversations with Professor Carlos Rincón in Berlin, Bogotá, Managua, and Cambridge about all sorts of topics, ranging from beauty queens and bullfights to memories of his childhood in Las Aguas neighborhood in Bogotá, opened my eyes to the importance of daily life to understanding the country and its people. Gracias!

A special thank-you goes to my editor Theresa May at the University of Texas Press and to copy editor Rosemary Wetherold, as well as to illustrator Juana Medina, who created the beautiful image for the cover.

Without all of you, this book would not have been possible.

A GRINGA IN BOGOTÁ

Even back then, before the Internet, dvds, and cds, before the TransMilenio superbuses and the Unicentro mall, before the fall of the Berlin Wall and before 9/11, even back then, U.S. travellers avoided Colombia.

I wasn't one of them.

After five years working for newspapers in the United States, I had taken a year off to explore Latin America. Latin America was in my bones, even if it wasn't in my blood. My parents had spent their honeymoon in Havana and Cuba; my mother had yearned to be a high school Spanish teacher. During my college years, I lived in a Dominican neighborhood in New York to save money on rent and went frequently with my neighbors to the Dominican Republic. My first job after graduating from Columbia Graduate School of Journalism was covering the Cuban community in New Jersey.

I didn't know much about Colombia when I arrived in Medellín or precisely, Envigado, in late fall of 1975, after a couple of months in Central America. A few months before in Florida, I had met Elaine, a young Romance language professor from the University of California, and her friend Nena, a bullfighter. I didn't know then that "nena" was a generic nickname for "girl," and not a proper name, but I was fascinated by the idea of a woman bullfighter.

I took up their invitation to stay at their farm home in Envigado. People tell me that the town is now one more neighborhood of Medellín, but at the time, it was rural and isolated. I enjoyed the women's hospitality, but I am an urban soul. Medellín, even when we visited, seemed a bigger version of the cities in Central America. I was bored with beans and the bland saltless variety of small white arepa, the inevitable corn pancake served with the beans and rice. After a few days, I took off for Bogotá, where I had the names of three Honduran graduate students at the Javeriana University, given to me by mutual friends in Central America.

I called Adelita, María de la Cruz, and Honduras (named after her country), and they immediately invited me to stay with them in a student residence near the university. They were charming and intellectually stimulating and knew Bogotá well. Even though I spent much of my time alone while they were in classes, they told me where to go and what to do. They introduced me to a delicious chicken stew called *ajiaco* and the huge variety of exotic fruit drinks. They guided me to obscure bookstores and told me about out-of-the-way museums.

One late afternoon, just before the sky burst into its nightly explosion of pinks, oranges, and yellows, I was returning to the university residences, walking along the Séptima, Bogotá's main avenue. I had just visited a gigantic bookstore called Buchholz, floor after floor of books in the downtown area. I spent hours there and left smelling musty and feeling happy. As I strolled along the Séptima, suddenly there was an overwhelming smell of eucalyptus. The sun was beginning to set. To my right was a dense park of tall trees and grass with infinite shades of green. I felt a surge in my stomach, or perhaps it was in my soul. It was a feeling of love, a feeling of love like when you see a person and fall in love at first sight. Only it wasn't a person. It was a city.

Then it was time to leave. I couldn't stay forever. I was off on a year's trip around Latin America, and Buenos Aires and Brazil lay ahead. But first there was Cali, a tropical city in western Colombia. From Cali, I planned on going to the colonial city of Popayán and then on to Ecuador. Many of the travellers I met in Central America had already flown there, skipping over Colombia. I sadly said good-bye to the Hondurans and to my Bogotá and headed off.

What I had forgotten or didn't know in the first place was that a fair in Cali was about to take place, as it did every December. I couldn't find a hotel room. Everything was full, except for the most expensive hotels and the kind used by prostitutes and lowlifes. I couldn't afford the former and wasn't about to risk the latter. The Hondurans in Bogotá had lived in a student residence; perhaps there were similar ones in Cali, I thought. So I bought a newspaper, asked someone about good neighborhoods, and made my way to a promising residence.

A middle-aged woman with red hair opened the door. I offered her a month's rent for a week's stay. "How do I know you're not a drug trafficker?" she asked. I was startled. "Look at my face. Do I look like a drug trafficker? I'm a journalist." "But how do I know that?" she asked, stressing the word "know." Journalists didn't have professional identity cards, and my passport didn't indicate my profession; drug traffickers at the time were indeed young North Americans, and the drug of choice was marijuana.

She gave herself the answer. "There is a journalist staying here, and when he comes home, if he says 'yes,' it's yes, and if he says 'no,' it's no."

The gentleman, who actually worked in the classified ads department of the newspaper *El País*, came home, talked to me, and said, "Sí!" He invited me to the paper's offices the next day.

He gave me a tour of the newspaper and asked if I wanted to meet some *paisanos*—fellow countrymen. I didn't particularly want to, but I said yes to be polite. We walked into a small and rather dark office. Someone was sitting at an oversized desk and looked up and asked, "Are you looking for a job?" I wasn't, but to be polite, I said yes.

He asked me about my experience and then said a job was available as an editor of the *Cali Chronicle*, the English-language weekly published by the Cali newspaper. He said that I was certainly qualified.

"There's a serious problem though," he added, pausing.

"What?" I asked, thinking of the pay scale or visa problems.

He replied with a worried look on his face: "It's in Bogotá."

I have a gringa accent.

I call the dentist, a friend of a friend. She asks me if I am familiar with Bogotá and where the neighborhood Galerías is. "Por supuesto," I snap at her. Of course, I know where it is. "I thought you didn't know Bogotá because of your accent," she calmly replies.

I shop for handicrafts. Before I start to bargain, I establish my turf: "Is that the price with or without the accent?" I sometimes get a chuckle. Sometimes there's complete silence.

Taxis are the worst. I sometimes take *busetas* or the Trans-Milenio to avoid what feels like an interrogation. "Where are you from? Do you like it here? Are you married? Are your children Colombian?" At least the last question acknowledges that I might have been here a long time; maybe my gringa accent isn't so bad after all.

With friends and folks that might become friends, I explain about the *primera* and *segunda rondas*, my first and second phases of living in Colombia. It's actually pretty straightforward. I came in 1975 and ended up staying for almost ten years, working as a correspondent for different media such as the *National Catholic Reporter*, the *Miami Herald*, and *Time*. I never really wanted to leave Colombia, but *Time* sent me to wartime Managua, a story that was too important to turn down.

And over the years, I kept my ties with Colombia, returning every year or two, making new Colombian friends in Managua, Germany, and New York and eventually at Harvard University, where I've spent the last nine years.

I decided to apply for a Fulbright to Colombia, in part to consider whether I want to retire here, to try to understand what has happened to this country and this city in the past thirty years, to share in the war and peace, the dreams and nightmares, of my friends and my friends' children. Many of the people I now consider my friends in Colombia were toddlers when I lived here. I was twenty-eight when I arrived. I have never had children, but it is in Colombia that I feel the flow of generations most strongly.

But how can I tell all this to a taxi driver? He—for inevitably, it is a he—won't understand or won't care. Bogotá has undergone tremendous cultural changes: women marry and have children late or don't have them at all; the word "gay" has worked its way into common vocabulary and a certain acceptance; unmarried women and men live independently from their families, even if their families live here in Bogotá. That wasn't the case thirty years ago.

But I'm not sure that those cultural shifts have worked into the taxi driver set. And I feel enough of a strange fish with my relentless gringa accent that it has made me an inveterate liar (or a fanciful storyteller, if I want to be easier on myself). Sometimes I'm Colombian-born but raised in the United States; more often, I came here in my twenties—in 1975, to be exact—because of my Colombian boyfriend. I'm now a widow, and yes, I have two kids, both grown, a doctor and a petroleum engineer. I occasionally switch the professions and sexes of my kids. Mostly, I model my family on a dear friend's children, now in their thirties. I really did watch them grow up and have children of their own.

Sometimes I think my taxicab lies match my emotional truth more closely than the fact that I arrived here again last August. Sometimes it feels as if I never left. The taxi drivers spur me to reminisce, calling upon me to legitimate my lie as if it were a plagiarized doctoral thesis. I recall when Unicentro was built in the far north of the city, Bogotá's first mall; I remind them of when traffic was hectic and no one ever obeyed any sorts of rules; I complain that Bogotá has become a megacity with noise and air pollution that sprawls north, south, and west and creeps up the eastern mountains. I praise the TransMilenio, the superfast bus network that has transformed the city, and admire the way people now throw trash in trash bins rather than on the streets. Bogotá residents—wherever they are from—now feel like citizens of the city.

I feel out the taxi driver's political position on President Uribe's "democratic security" and recall the human rights abuses of the Turbay administration and later the tragic conflagration of the Palace of Justice following a guerrilla takeover. I remember when the Candelaria, now mostly an upscale and bohemian colonial sector, was all *inquilinatos*, squalid boardinghouses. And I recall how my downtown apartment on Calle 19 was right in front of a building called Cudecom that had been moved the previous year in a technical feat of engineering. It wasn't a great neighborhood, but most people expected gentrification—as eventually happened in the Candelaria. Now my former neighborhood is a *zona de tolerancia*, a red-light district. The taxi drivers inevitably empathize.

Sometimes they are from elsewhere, and I find myself telling them Bogotá history. Sometimes they are in their thirties or forties, and I am recalling their childhood years. And sometimes they remember along with me. I try to get them to tell their stories. They gave been driving for years; they used to drive a bus, but now they drive a cab; they are salesmen, engineers, small factory owners, fathers of children going to college in Bogotá from elsewhere in the country; they are the sons of peasants and the fathers of students. They are victims of violence and weavers of dreams.

I leave the taxis with my emotional truths and factual lies. I leave the taxis with the history of this city and the history of this country all feeling like one unbroken thread, a shared experience. I still have my gringa accent.

Life and Rules

Colombia may be the most beautiful country I know. It certainly is the most diverse.

That accidental conversation in the offices of *El País* led to more than nine years of explorations of Colombia's nooks and crannies, its towering Andes, its sweltering jungles, its tropical Caribbean. It led to lifelong friendships. The job at the *Cali Chronicle* also led to correspondent jobs for different U.S. media. I covered the rise of the M-19 guerrillas and the takeover of the Dominican Embassy in Bogotá. I wrote about the role of the Catholic Church, and I penned articles about escalating human rights abuses.

I used every excuse I could to get into the countryside, to report on the lepers in the colony of Agua de Dios that had their own post office system so no one would get sick from the stamps; the descendants of rebel slaves in Palenque whose knowledge of traditional martial arts had produced world champion boxers; the black-faced indigenous people of the Cabo de la Vela in the Guajira Peninsula whose lives would be changed by a coal mine; gold craftsmen in Mompós, along the Magdalena River; nuns in the Sierra Nevada who administered to me my very first cup of coca tea to ward off altitude sickness.

Stories were everywhere, tucked into ravishingly spectacular landscapes. In many ways, Colombia was exotic. But beyond exotic, it had become home.

The most visible guerrilla group was the urban-based M-19. Bogotá became increasingly militarized, and the threat of violence was always there like a steady hum. In the countryside, older guerrilla groups such as the FARC (Revolutionary Armed Forces of Colombia) were mostly forgotten, engaging in sporadic and localized activities. The Colombian government became involved with the peace process in Central America. And, increasingly, I split my time between Central America, the hot spot of the cold war, and Colombia—home.

Eventually, I left for Managua and then Berlin, New York, and, finally, Cambridge. I transitioned from being a reporter to being an editor and a professor. And yet Colombia never became part of my past with journalistic jaunts and evocative experiences shelved in the recesses of memory. I visited on a yearly basis, sometimes more frequently.

In New York and Boston, I visited the Colombian communities, ate arepas and *bandeja paisa*, read the newspapers, and watched the occasional soap opera like *Betty la Fea*. I became fascinated with the Colombian community in East Boston, most of whom hailed from the same small town in Colombia, Don Matías. I became an active member of the Colombian Colloquium, a Harvard-MIT–based group of students and professionals eager to find peaceful solutions for the country.

During my frequent trips to Colombia since 1984, I have often thought that Bogotá provides an archaeology of my past, a generational and geographic span that I find no place else. My trips have mostly been limited to Bogotá, constricted by time and the desire to see my friends. With some exceptions, my trips have centered around Christmas, that extended time of year when work stops and peace most often reigns.

I've sometimes asked myself where the war is, the war we discuss so incessantly up at Harvard. I ask myself how Colombia has changed, and how I have changed, and whether we have changed together. Or is a Christmas vacation with friends in Bogotá an oasis, an illusion?

I'm always asked, "But is it safe?" and sometimes "Isn't there a war going on here?" or just "What's Colombia like?" I feel a bit like a schizophrenic in my answers, just as I do with the taxi drivers. Nothing is quite all true. I could tell them that Colombia is beautiful and filled with mountains and beaches and a huge range of biodiversity, that it has produced Shakira and Juanes and Botero and Gabriel García Márquez and, for that matter, Juan Valdez. Or I could tell them that Colombia has the world's greatest number of internal war refugees after the Sudan, that drug traffic has fueled paramilitary forces and guerrilla groups, that the war has spanned two generations and probably won't stop anytime soon.

I remember that during a recent plane trip from Pasto, in the south of the country, to Bogotá, my companion, a Colombian working for the Norwegian Refugee Council, complained about a recent BBC program that talked about the vast improvement in urban life in Bogotá. "They talk about that while our towns and villages are bleeding to death," she scowled.

I kept silent. Of course, what she said was true: the rural areas around Pasto were subject to violence, fumigation, and displacement. But yet, for many people in the United States and Europe, that's Colombia's only reality. I wanted to tell her that it was important to talk about the TransMilenio, to talk about the positive, without denying the war.

I try to puzzle out how the war is so often absent and yet it is always present, an invisible war that suddenly becomes visible, a war of many generations that has embedded itself into the Colombian soul—and perhaps into my own. I will myself to understand, but holidays are always too short and self-enclosed.

That's why I decided to apply for a Fulbright, with my official goal being to help the National University of Colombia set up its master's program in journalism. Unofficially, I want to figure out my life and to understand this city, this country, that has become my love.

I suppose I could have done it by re-creating my life as a journalist, reexploring the country's many corners, chasing after battles and massacres. I suppose that would be one way to do it. And yet, I constantly remind myself, I am fifty-nine, not twenty-eight. My value here is as a journalism professor, helping to form young journalists, rather than to try to be one of them. As for reexploring the country, I would be spreading myself too thin, not giving myself time to understand how it really feels to live daily life in Bogotá's capital city.

I teach my journalism students to listen to ordinary people, to tell tales about ordinary lives. So I'm setting out to write about my experience this year. I want to treat myself as an ordinary person, if not a typical one. I want to listen to this city and hear what it says to me. I want to listen to Bogotá, take its pulse, and use my experience here as a prism through which to understand the country.

I want to focus on *lo cotidiano*, the everyday, and see what happens. I am a middle-aged, middle-class woman, a gringa who loves this country and feels rooted here. I want to walk out of my house and see what I see. I will not go looking for the war. I will travel insofar as my fellowship generates invitations. I will not isolate myself in the ivory tower, but I will not go out of my way to seek poverty and crisis. I hope I am not becoming jaded. I make these rules about my stay. But maybe, then, sometimes I will break them too.

Looking for María

Her name was María de Ostos, and she was a short, chubby, energetic woman with two winsome daughters, Janet and Olga. She worked as my maid in Bogotá for most of my *primera ronda* in Colombia. Sometimes she'd invite me to her home, a humble abode on an unpaved street in northern Bogotá, surrounded by brick quarries and smelling of fresh air and eucalyptus. After I left Bogotá, we kept in touch for a few years through postcards. During my short jaunts to the city over the years, I never tried to find her. She had no telephone, no street address, and time was usually too short to venture out to her distant barrio.

Back in Bogotá for my Fulbright year, I was convinced that I would never be able to locate her. Yet I decided to set out on the Lijacá-Usaquén bus that wends its way up the Séptima, 140 blocks north of where I live. The only note I had in my address book is "get off at 166th St. and walk up five blocks until you see a house with a white wall in front of it."

La Séptima, as Seventh Avenue is always called, wends its way through Bogotá like an ambling river, passing through rich and poor neighborhoods, the restaurants from Pasto, Medellín, and Cartagena, passing by the beggars, the *desplazados* (displaced) from all over Colombia, the lawyers, the doctors, the university students, the schoolkids, the business executives. La Séptima ebbs and flows and changes, and like a river, its presence is a point of constant reference. The bus runs up the avenue, and I stare out, watching the city's transformations.

The minute I saw the curved, paved street stretching into the hills from the Séptima, I remembered the route. Only before, the pavement stopped just after the main highway. Now it continued all the way up. Off the side of the street, fancy new high-rise apartment buildings were being constructed.

Indeed, throughout the bus trip, I was startled by how the city had expanded northward since I lived here, towering red brick buildings in guarded apartment complexes, fast-food restaurants like Charlie's Roastbeef and Dunkin' Donuts, shiny new shopping centers with huge ads for Levi's and cell phones. As the bus lurched into the 140s, I could see ramshackle housing with tin roofs, stones on top to keep them from blowing away, tiny houses stretching up the sides of the green mountains.

I remembered how, when I used to visit María, I wondered why it was the poor who lived on the sides of the mountain with fresh air and a spectacular view of the city. In most cities I knew, it was the rich who enjoyed fresh air and scenery. Now, all along the bus route, I had seen elegant new housing along the sides of the mountains, stretching up and up where the poor had used to live. Only after more than a hundred blocks did the poor once again take possession of the hillsides.

Before I embarked on the journey, I had worried that the address I had wasn't precise enough or that María had moved elsewhere. As I watched the urban landscape, I began to fret that development might have taken over the entire neighborhood, brick factories churned into apartment complexes. Other than the high-rises being constructed near the main avenue, María's neighborhood was an improved version of its old self. Small stores selling cell phone minutes and freshly baked bread abounded. Houses that had been shambles of bricks with tin roofs had evolved into solid brick structures.

I walk up and up. I don't remember feeling so winded and fatigued on the long climb, but I'm twenty-odd years older and not as used to the altitude either. I keep asking in the little stores about the family. I'm told that the Ostoses live further up and that they also have a *tienda*, a little store. The shopkeepers know María and her family. I'm going to find her.

I tentatively enter what seems to be a large private house with a little store. No one seems to be attending the store, so I call out, "Does anyone here know María de Ostos?" I don't think I'm in the right place; I haven't seen a white wall, and probably need to keep on climbing. Two young women—well, actually, not that young—start yelling, "June, June, June! It's June!" Another, older woman, about my age, looks at me, and the daughters insist, "It's June," and they all fall on me in excitement.

The daughters have all had children, and now María has several grandchildren and a couple of great-grandchildren. They catch me up on their lives. María runs the store and works as an occasional day maid and makes jewelry, as well as raising chickens and renting out rooms in the large house, which has expanded at least threefold since I last visited.

Olga is currently unemployed but usually works as a maid, and she dreams of going to the United States. Janet keeps an elderly woman company, but she has also worked in nongovernmental agencies, and it shows. She is verbal and bright and interested in life; so is her ten-year-old daughter, Erika.

Janet reminds me of María as a younger woman, although she is far more literate and worldly. Yet María, my maid, always surprised me with her wisdom. One of the reasons I remember her so vividly is that I often incorporate her narrative in my journalism classes. When María used to work for me, I would travel frequently to El Salvador, in the midst of its civil war.

One day she asked me, "Doña June, aren't you afraid when you go to El Salvador?"

"No, María," I replied. "Well, when I'm on the plane, I always feel a bit jittery, but when I get there and the discotheques are playing their music and people are eating in restaurants and the shopping malls are filled, I forget about being afraid. It all feels so normal."

"No, Doña June," she protested. "That's in the city. In the country, there is fear."

I paused. María was right. When journalists went out to the countryside, we were constantly afraid, afraid of mines and ambushes and crossfire, stumbling into towns and villages that were still mourning the warm bodies of children and women, hearing the tales of massacres and midnight raids. María was right, but I didn't know how she knew.

"You're right, María, but how do you know that? Some television program?"

"No," she explained. "When I was a young girl, we lived in Boyacá during the time of La Violencia. It was dangerous for the adults or the older girls and boys to get the milk in the morning, so they sent us children down the road to get the milk at dawn. And we saw bodies along the road, bodies that had been cut up in all sorts of nasty ways, some without heads. But we were children and we tried to contain our fear and just get the milk and come back.

"Later, we moved to Bogotá, and there everything that had happened in the countryside was just like a dream, or maybe I should say a nightmare. There was no fear, just the memory of fear."

María, with her story of her childhood, enlightened for me forever my experience of Central America, and of Colombia too. I sit in her kitchen now, decades later, and think how much she taught me. Janet and Olga remind me that I taught them "that song," and burst out in a chorus of "Ee-aye-ee-aye-oh," a fairly good rendering of "Ol' McDonald Had a Farm." Not a fair trade, I think, but they seem to cherish the memory.

I ask about the neighborhood, and the family's comments confirm my impression. It is "tranquilo" and the people are "solidaria," a quiet and collaborative neighborhood. I admit that I emptied out my purse and only brought the essentials with me. They laugh. I ask about the war: do they feel it in their community in some way, *desplazados* maybe? They say the war is far away, that it's not here in the neighborhood. Janet muses, "I felt it in my work." She tells me that she worked with many orphans, children of addicts, of AIDS victims, of *desplazados*. The children would tell her, "I saw my father murdered by men who came in the middle of the night" or "My parents dragged me from my bed at three a.m. and said people were coming to get us and we had to run and leave our cows and chickens behind." The war is not invisible for Janet, even though she never experienced it, as her mother did, and even though her neighborhood is peaceful.

María invites me up the barranca out the back of her house. Janet and Olga and Erika help me scramble up. The brick factories are gone, but there are still rough mountain crags. We pass María's chickens and a curuba tree and a patch of squash plants and look out over the city, extending north and west and south, a huge, rambling city that is so much larger than the last time I enjoyed this view. The wood oven has moved out here, replaced inside by a modern gas stove. Sometimes they still have barbecues here with this enviable view.

Janet and I continue to chat. She is still talking about her work with one of the nongovernmental agencies. "I felt so sorry for the children, for the orphans," she tells me. "You ask me about the war. There are many wars, I think. The war of the paramilitaries and the war of the narcos and the war of the people who abuse their children and have no values. And I wonder what war is worse. Maybe the war of no values, because that will go on and on and on."

We stare out into the horizon of the almost endless city. I can't help thinking, like mother, like daughter.

View from My Window

The heavy clouds of mist drift across the Andes, floating past my window, obscuring my view of the white Monserrate church shrine. The mist hangs over the mountains like a Japanese cloud painting, and I see the muted green of tall pine trees peeking through. The Virgin of Guadalupe crowns a neighboring mountaintop; she too is lost in the mist.

Birds soar past my window in winged flocks or solo. I watch them as they gracefully head for points north or south. For me, they are birds without a name, nature's creatures amid tall skyscrapers.

The view from my downtown apartment is constantly changing. By the afternoon, Monserrate, 3,200 meters above sea level, has turned a verdant green. The sky is a transparent blue. The shimmering sunlit intensity recalls the Technicolor of early color films, turning my view into a picture postcard. I watch the cable car move slowly from the bottom of the mountain to the church sanctuary, and every once in a while, especially on a Sunday, I can see tiny figures as they climb on foot in pilgrimage toward the shrine.

Although I live downtown, right across the street from Colpatria, Colombia's tallest building, my apartment faces the mountains and the Parque de la Independencia, Independence Park. Large windows frame the rooms of my apartment, and as I write, I watch the shifting scenery.

Independence Park, the view on the left side of my windows, is a medley of different greens, forested with weeping willows, eucalyptus, pine, and rubber trees, as well as Chinese chestnut trees known as *urapanes*. From my window, through the trees I can barely see the newly renovated Quiosco de la Luz, the Kiosk of Light—a fanciful octagon decked out in neoclassical ornamentation celebrating the four seasons, an exact copy of the music belvedere constructed in Versailles by Marie Antoinette in the eighteenth century. In my first month here, I've watched the abandoned kiosk, often used as a urinal by the homeless, emerge as a fanciful work of art, a remodeling of this remnant of the park's 1910 agro-industrial fair.

This view from my window is in the news, as Bogotá and Colombia look toward the future. Independence Park, I learn, was

Bogotá's first modern urban park, inaugurated in 1883. In 1910 the fair became the city's symbol of modernity, an opportunity to introduce new ideas and technology, a symbol of national pride. The cement used in the kiosk was for the first time ever Colombian cement, and the kiosk disguised the electric generation used to light up the fair.

An exhibit at the nearby Bogotá Museum describes the fair's ample pavilions: industry, machines, farm animals, fine arts, Egyptian arts and history, and light. They are all gone now, these odes to progress, except for the imaginative little kiosk that lights up at night and shines into my study.

Yet the charming kiosk peeping through the trees is also a monument to remembrance and forgetting, I learn from the exhibit. The fair sought to celebrate progress, to leave behind the recent War of the Thousand Days and the painful U.S-fomented secession of Panama. The civil war between Liberals and Conservatives, lasting from 1899 to 1902, resulted in 60,000 to 130,000 deaths, extensive property damage, and economic havoc.

Now when I look at the illuminated monument out my window, I sometimes think of this other war, this oft-invisible war, that I am trying so hard to understand, today's silent dance of remembrance and forgetting.

My eyes rest on some puffy white clouds drifting past Guadalupe. Mostly my view is to enjoy, not to think. Nestled into the mountains and pines and green Chinese chestnut trees are tall buildings, melting into the leafy panorama. The Torres del Parque, the Torres Blancas, and the KLM Towers remind me that I am in a modern city, but they blend with nature in a way that most skyscrapers never do.

I look down on some of Bogotá's finest cultural monuments, the Museum of Modern Art and the Biblioteca Nacional, the National Library. The neighboring movie multiplex, the Embajador, also beckons, even though I have to crane my neck to see it.

One day, I notice a poor barrio right next to the Torres Blancas, the white towers that were one of the first modern apartment buildings for the middle class and intellectuals. The neighborhood obviously had been there all along, an integral part of my verdant green view, but I just never noticed.

The mountainside houses look ramshackle, with red brick and zinc roofs, and I decide I will go investigate. I empty my pocketbook, wear a jacket with hidden pockets, and leave my apartment key with the doorman. Curious, he asks where I am going. I tell him I am going up to the poor barrio I can see from my window, and ask him if he has ever been there.

"No," he says, and warns me that he has heard that robbers attack pilgrims who have chosen the neighborhood as an alternative route to the Monserrate shrine. I decide not to go for now. I ask him if he knows the name of the barrio. "Yes," he says. "It's La Paz"—peace.

It is night now, and again I look at the view from my window. Monserrate and Guadalupe twinkle in the distance. The kiosk of light shines through the trees, now black leafy shadows. And the barrio of La Paz disappears from sight in the enveloping darkness.

Dreaming of Journalism

I love teaching journalism. I think of myself as a midwife who helps students realize their writing skills and their voice. And I believe that journalism, even though much maligned, is a search for truth. And that by searching for truth, one searches for justice.

When I applied for the Fulbright to come to Colombia, I had hoped to teach in the National University's first class in a newly designed undergraduate journalism program. María Jimena Duzán, a columnist for *El Tiempo*, was involved in the planning process, and from the outside at least, it seemed as if the project was full steam ahead. On a short trip to Bogotá, I talked to the then rector Marco Palacios, who was promoting the project.

I dreamed. I could return to this city, where I had spent so many formative years, and teach what I know about journalism.

It didn't happen that way. Palacios resigned. The university was convulsed with protests about a proposed academic reform that students considered "neoliberal." Someone in the university administration decided the journalism program should be a master's, not an undergraduate degree. I got the Fulbright. But there was no program in which to teach.

I was asked by the vice-rector's office if I could design a journalism program. I've never done that before, although I've been close to the formation of the master's program at Harvard Extension School and carefully watched the turf wars at Columbia Journalism School, my alma mater, over whether to institute a two-year program. I decided to take on the challenge.

Over the years, I've been very close to Colombian journalists. When I worked as a foreign correspondent here in the midseventies and eighties, I enjoyed getting to know the local reporters. I admired the writing and reporting of many of them and was sometimes stunned at how radio journalists managed to get to important sources on the spot.

Once, while visiting Miami, I heard a news flash on the radio in my rental car that a hijacked Spanish airline had been forced to land in Miami to refuel before heading on to Cuba. The news bulletin was of great practical interest to me because I had a flight later in the day and needed to know if the airport was closed. I kept switching from station to station, both English and Spanish. Either there was no news about the hijacking or the same old tired news that I had heard on the first station. Finally, I heard a news report that excited me: a radio journalist was interviewing the pilot in the hijacked plane's cockpit. I waited for station identification, thinking this was a particularly aggressive Miami Cuban station. Instead, it was the Miami correspondent for Colombia's Caracol Radio. I shouldn't have been surprised.

Talent abounds. When I returned to New York after eighteen years abroad in Latin America and Europe, I became involved in a mentoring program at Columbia Graduate School of Journalism. And my mentees were both Colombian: Margarita Martínez, who became an Associated Press reporter in Bogotá and then the producer of *La Sierra*, an acclaimed documentary on a paramilitary-controlled slum in Medellín; and Juanita León, editor of lasillavacia.com, an independent online political news magazine, as well as a book author.

Talent abounds, but I can't help thinking that Margarita and Juanita—both lawyers by training—might not have developed their journalism careers in the same way without their studies at Columbia. What I wanted to do was to develop a program for the National University that would allow the Margaritas and Juanitas (and the Pedros and Pablos) to get a top-notch journalism education at home.

Over the years, much of the pool of Colombian talent has been drained by assassinations and forced exile. Even when journalists felt they could return home safely, they often didn't. They had established their roots elsewhere, in Spain, in Mexico, and in the United States. Journalists in the provinces face the greatest dangers now, often caught between the crossfire of guerrillas and paramilitary. And they are precisely the journalists with the least training. In 2006 alone the New York–based Committee to Protect Journalists (CPJ) documented six cases of provincial journalists forced to flee their homes because of threats and intimidation.

It's not just a thing of the past. Pedro Antonio Cárdenas Cáceres, director of the biweekly *La Verdad* in Honda, a sweltering town on the Magdalena River about three hours from here, was one of those journalists who left and returned.

But he fled to Bogotá with his family after finding funeral flowers in front of his house two days in a row, he told CPJ. Cárdenas believes that the threats are linked to recent investigative stories on local government corruption.

The painful stories go on and on. As I update and revise this essay, I find that the Committee to Protect Journalists called on Colombian authorities to fully investigate death threats against a provincial journalist who criticized a local mayor.

Marcos Perales Mendoza, editor of the weekly regional newspaper *Portada* in the northeastern city of Bucaramanga, has already been given a bulletproof vest and a two-way police radio by the Interior Ministry. But he says authorities are not investigating who is behind the death threats that began in May last year when he published stories on government corruption in the river port city of Barrancabermeja.

Two local journalists fled the region in January after reporting on paramilitary activities, according to CPJ. Jenny Manrique, coordinator of a supplement for the Bucaramanga-based daily *Vanguardia Liberal*, left after receiving death threats for reporting on abuses by paramilitary forces.

A prominent radio journalist who interviewed accused drug traffickers awaiting extradition to the United States told CPJ he received an e-mail warning to leave Colombia within three days or face "consequences without precedent for your children and family." Herbin Hoyos Medina is still in Colombia but told CPJ he was considering leaving. I decide to stop revising; the numbers keep escalating and the names proliferating.

Twenty-eight Colombian journalists have been slain in the past decade, although deadly violence has tapered off in the past two years, according to the CPJ. In 2005 only one Colombian journalist was murdered. But the CPJ notes, "Minimal state presence in vast areas of the country continues to leave journalists at the mercy of illegal armed groups. Journalists in Bogotá and other large urban centers work more freely than colleagues in the country's interior, but they, too, face pressure and intimidation. Government officials have sometimes contributed to the climate of fear by accusing journalists of having ties to the guerrillas."

I know that a journalism program won't resolve these problems. I can only believe that a solid formation and accurate reporting are a journalist's best defenses. And I can help establish ties between this fledgling journalism program and organizations in the United States that specialize in safety and in combating impunity and trauma.

I'm not sure if I'm dreaming. But at least I will try.

It's a bit earlier in the morning than I like to be up and about. But my friend Angelika Rettberg of the Universidad de los Andes' Political Science Department is moderating a panel titled "Ciudadanía y Conflicto"—Citizenship and Conflict. Friendship takes precedence over an extra hour under the covers on a chilly Bogotá morning.

Lots of people are on the street. Two office workers giggle over something or other as they wait for a green light. Students scurry to classes. A well-dressed man chats with a newspaper vendor. A homeless man is still sleeping on the corner, wrapped in rags and tucked into a cardboard box.

I stop for a quick coffee at a bakery. The store is filled with people of all ages, drinking coffee, eating cheese empanadas, and doughnut-like jelly-filled pastries called *roscones*, chatting and laughing. The displaced people, war refugees, aren't out on the street yet with their homemade posters and hungry children. From my apartment to Los Andes, a twenty-minute walk, I usually see two or three families later in the day. The war is always somewhere else, and these families are a reminder of its existence. I've been back in Bogotá now for a couple of months, and I'm always struck by how normal, even upbeat, things are. It's apparently not just my perception. The Dutch World Database of Happiness ranked Colombia in fourth place last year.

That's on my mind as the panel begins. The idea, Angelika explains, is to show the relationship between citizenship and conflict *desde la cotidianidad*, from the perspective of daily life. She adds that one of the least-studied dramas is the ability of citizens to coexist with violence. One learns not to go down certain streets, not to notice the bomb-sniffing dogs in the supermarkets, not to carry more money or credit cards than necessary, to be on the lookout. Citizens have been born into and have grown up in violence, she points out.

I'm not a fan of statistics, but the poll statistics woke me up. In a third of the communities polled, there were testimonies of massacres, and 61 percent of those polled said the armed conflict had affected their life negatively. Yet those polled consistently insisted that social problems and corruption concerned them more than armed violence.

Almost half said that they or someone in their close family had been kidnapped, displaced, raped, tortured, or killed in the past four years. "Close" family was also carefully defined to include only siblings, children, parents, uncles and aunts, and first cousins, to avoid "extended family" interpretation. The four-year limit was also interesting, since it encompassed most of President Uribe's term, in which perceptions are that the situation is improving.

The poll question rattled in my head as I walked home, past the bakery, past the fish restaurants and the people forming lines to pay their telephone bills, past the family of displaced people who had placed their cardboard sign next to a *canasta* (basket) for coins, past the shops that feature cell phone calls by the minute, past all the sights and sounds of the everyday.

I was a block away from home, just outside Koko Rico, the rotisserie chicken restaurant, when a photographer friend spotted me. I was absorbed in the poll question and getting home for lunch. We chatted for a few minutes, and I figured I might as well ask the question. I wasn't expecting much of anything; the war always seemed to be someplace else.

"Yes," he said, looking a bit startled. "My grandmother was kidnapped three years ago."

His eighty-some-year-old grandmother lived in a house out on a finca, a country farm just outside of Bogotá. She loved to garden and to tend to the animals. And then one day an armed group, probably guerrillas, carried her away and demanded ransom. Negotiations began, and finally the grandmother was released, tossed onto the side of the road, wrapped up in white sheets. She now lives in the city with her family and hasn't been the same in her head since, he said.

He didn't tell the story back then because he was afraid it might break off negotiations, and he usually doesn't tell it now because it is too painful and somehow irrelevant. Life goes on. Yet he stands on the sidewalk for fifteen minutes, or maybe it was twenty, and tells the wrenching story in graphic detail. Around me are all the stores and restaurants and sites of my daily life, my daily peaceful life in Bogotá, and now the conflict is here, an insidious and silent reality.

We say good-bye. I am shaken. Surely this was an exception to the rule. Here was someone I knew fairly well, and yet the story had been invisible. My friend is what I would call a happy person; he likes to party and drink and be creative with his photography.

I return to my building, and a neighbor enters at the same time, inviting me to a prelunch coffee. I accept, glad not to be alone for a while. I tell him about the panel and repeat the question, only I forget the part about the four-year limit. My neighbor tells how his family was caught up in the violence between the Liberals and the Conservatives in the last century and had to flee their little town in Santander for the provincial capital of Bucaramanga, and then to the capital city of Bogotá. The violence changed his family's life, displacing it from its regional roots. By the time I realize he is talking about a more distant past, I can't stop the flow of the story.

Finally, I add, meekly, "And in the last four years? That's actually how the poll defined the question."

And off he went again, with the story of a landowner tied to the paramilitaries who had threatened him after he had denounced a polluting septic tank to local authorities. The tank, which he considered a health hazard, was on the property next to his shared weekend house a few hours from Bogotá. The death threats were anonymous but persistent. He has not returned for more than a year.

I went upstairs and made a light lunch. I couldn't eat. I wondered how many invisible stories are floating around my normal, daily life. I don't feel like asking the poll question again. But I know I will.

Life on Movie Row

I live on movie row, the concrete intersection between celluloid fantasy and gritty reality.

My apartment looks down on one side on the Embajador, an elegant old movie house that has been chopped up into several small viewing rooms with first-run movies. On the other side, my apartment looks over the *cinemateca*, the art movie theatre, in the Museum of Modern Art, affectionately known as MAMBO. Just a block away is the Cinemateca Distrital, another art movie house, and across the street is the Opera Plaza, tucked into a small worn-down mall with an ample food court. Not to mention the cine-clubs run by the universities around my house. It's a movie lover's feast.

There are most always lines: gray-haired gentlemen with mustaches and wool trousers that have seen better days, young couples with purple hair and blue jeans, university students, a heady mix of young and old.

Crowds flock to see *Crash* and *Brokeback Mountain* and *The Da Vinci Code*, Hollywood blockbusters with Spanish-language subtitles. But there are also lines to see Jim Jarmusch's *Ghost Dog* at the MAMBO *cinemateca* or his more recent *Broken Flowers* at the Embajador. Festivals flourish: retrospectives of Woody Allen, German films, Russian films, zombie films, terror films, romance films. And always the lines.

The moviegoers aren't flocking to just foreign films. Colombian films are abundant and increasingly sophisticated: films like

Rosario Tijeras, a cruel depiction of the effects of the Colombian drug trade, and *María, llena eres de gracia* (Maria Full of Grace), the heart-wrenching tale of a pregnant Colombian flower-worker who tries to make her fortune as a drug mule. And for every film that deals with the drug trade and violence, there's one that renders the other side of Colombian life, the sad and the funny, like *Mi abuelo, mi papá y yo*, Dago García's tragicomic three-generational love story.

Last year eight new Colombian releases hit the market. More than a million spectators (1,053,030) viewed *Rosario Tijeras*, a co-production by Mexican director Emilio Maillé. According to the Ministry of Culture, three other Colombian films garnered more than 200,000 spectators each: *Mi abuelo, mi papá y yo; Perder es cuestión de método*, by Sergio Cabrera; and *Sumas y restas*, by Víctor Gaviria.

This film enthusiasm isn't new. Indeed, I remember, about thirty years ago I was a juror at the yearly Cartagena Film Festival, a tropical and somewhat lightweight version of Cannes that has never quite taken off, despite the splendid colonial setting. Bogotá also now has its own yearly festival, more of a celebration of film than the competitive, showy atmosphere of Cartagena.

If I were to judge by what I see, Colombia is movie territory. Census statistics remind me that only 3 percent of the population can afford a movie or theatre ticket, not to mention popcorn and babysitters, since Bogotá is no longer a mecca of live-in maids. Movie theatres install cafés and sell passes with heavy discounts to encourage moviegoing. DVDs, many of them pirated, are stiff competition, sold readily on the streets by vendors with the lyrical cry of "Pe-lí-cu-las, pe-lí-cu-las . . ."

Still, I've promised myself to write of what I see. And what I see are movie fanatics, eager to take in first-run movies and to enjoy the old and esoteric. Again, memories creep in, trying to remind me how movies were in Bogotá when I lived here the first time. And I remember another movie theatre that would have been a stone's throw from my apartment: the Olimpia, right along the side of Calle 26, next to a European-style bakery and coffeehouse. It could hold up to five thousand people, and I don't ever remember it being full. Both the bakery and the movie house are gone now, replaced by a cafeteria and a leather shop. At least, I think that's exactly where the 1912 theatre used to be. I have walked that block countless times in my Fulbright year to get to the TransMilenio.

And thinking of the Olimpia, I become aware of the architectural whispers of the movie past. There's the elegant Faenza, now being remodeled into a university auditorium, and the cavernous Metropol, right next to the Embajador and serving as an occasional concert hall and discotheque, and the stately Mogador with its art deco flourishes and still serving as a movie theatre, but for pornographic films. I talk to a sympathetic ticket teller for about ten minutes before the X-rated film is slated to roll, and she leads me on a tour of the building. The theatre is cavernous, with more than a thousand seats on the first level and a balcony, now closed, above. The floor creaks, and my impromptu tour guide warns me to watch out for holes. The green leather seats are worn and torn, but I envy the impressive "bones" of the theatre, with its Italian marble, high ceilings, and ornate decorations. The Embajador must have looked this way too, before it was carved up into small personality-free screening rooms.

The ticket taker reminisces about the Mexican movies that used to fill the theatre and others like it; Mexican actors and *charro* singers Cantinflas, Tin Tan, Capulina, and Vicente Fernández catered to the popular tastes of the public. Indeed, I vaguely remember another downtown movie house called Cine México. Some of these movie houses are now porno film houses like the Mogador; others are evangelical churches, and some have been leveled into parking lots.

As much as I live on movie row, downtown used to be movie paradise.

And yet the paradise, as always here, is relative. I never used to be able to see first-run films. My friends in the States were always writing me about films that took six months to a year to get here, or never came at all.

Last year 182 new releases were exhibited, 110 from the United States, 72 from other countries, and 8 Colombian films, according to the Ministry of Culture. And 16,313,814 moviegoers went to commercial theatres, not counting the cine-clubs and all the other offbeat venues. That's twice the population of Bogotá.

It's late afternoon movie time on an intermittently sunny day, and I look down from my window at the Embajador. There are lines, as usual. I muse on why so many people go to the movies — well, at least the people I can see out my window. Is it mere escapism, a "fool's paradise" to which people resort, a way of escaping the war refugees on the street and the nightly gore of the television news? Is it a way of being in the outside world, a way to create bridges with New York and Los Angeles and Buenos Aires? Is it just something to do, like going to a concert or a party? I think about Dago García's phrase in an interview I read about his recent movie: "What's clear to me is that people from all social classes are buying emotions [when they go to the movies]."

Maybe that's why I like the movies also. I love to go to the movies with friends, but I recently learned that it's also entertaining to bop down to the Embajador and pick out a seat that's just three rows from the movie screen, immersing me in the sights and sounds. Colombians prefer seats that are further away from the screen, and I learned the hard way that *preferencial* seats, for which one pays a higher price, are actually located in the back of the theatre. It's all in the perspective.

The last film I saw at the Embajador was a German flick called *Los edukadores*, a film about idealistic and rebel youth who go around breaking into rich people's homes, moving furniture, and leaving slogans like "Your Days of Plenty Are Numbered." When a cell phone is left behind, reentry to get it back results in the impromptu kidnapping of a wealthy businessman who, as the story emerges, may or may not have been a leader in the 1968 student uprisings. My heart went out to the idealistic youths, who more or less stumbled into the kidnapping and were making the best of it in a German national park. I also felt a teeny bit of sympathy for the businessman, for whom ideals were a long-ago remnant of the past. And, of course, I wondered if the same had happened to me, sitting in this movie house when I could be teaching kids to read in Ciudad Bolívar instead of spending on the movie ticket what a minimum-wage worker earns in a day. But those thoughts were momentaneous, as I cheered on the idealistic trio and hoped they would come out of the situation unscathed (they did).

I saw the film alone but later compared notes with a Colombian friend in her thirties. She loved the film, and she too identified with the youngsters. But, she added, her parents hated the way the film ended. "Why?" I asked, since the businessman also came out of the ordeal safe and sound. "Because it's a kidnapping," she replied. "And in Colombia, when the kidnappers get away, that's a bad thing."

And perhaps that was my answer about the movies. In Colombia, as Dago García pointed out, film is about the emotions, and with the emotions, the history and reality of the internal conflict are never quite parked at the door.

Redprodepaz: Knitting Peace

The river flowed red with blood.

I couldn't get the image out of my head. I watched the community organizer as she tried to stop her tears and continue to explain her youth project. And she repeated, "The river flowed red with blood."

The traffic is flowing outside. Car brakes are screeching and pierce through the double glass on the windows. For a moment, I hear nothing from the Bogotá streets, concentrating in the image of a far-off massacre.

We are gathered here in the Club de Ejecutivos in downtown Bogotá, a stone's throw from my apartment, to discuss peace and development narratives from around the country. The group is called Redprodepaz, and the narrative project is sponsored through the Universidad de los Andes. The purpose is to strengthen civil society in Colombia. I've been accompanying the group in my role as a Fulbright professor, but even before this year, I've heard many of its members participate as part of a Harvard project called Beyond Armed Actors.

The group is working with a series of alliances between community organizations, petroleum foundations, and universities. Caught between war and peace, poverty and development, the organizations are working in very concrete ways to tip the balance in their favor. Some work with youth to create opportunities to stem recruitment by paramilitary and guerrillas. Others teach literacy, both in the cities and in the countryside. That means not just teaching to read and write but also teaching for democracy, with emphasis on citizens' values.

I ask one of the participants what difference demobilizing the paramilitary has made, and she points to common crime and political power. She wrinkles her face and says, "It's just the same."

The war is a moving chessboard, and as I sit in the conference room, listening to narrative after narrative, I hear a central theme: *el problema del estómago*, the problem of hunger. Nothing will change until something is done about poverty.

Solutions aren't that simple. In a program in the Arauca region of Colombia, for example, a community organization started a literacy program, as well as providing training and tools for a barbershop. The barbershop was highly successful for a while, bringing a source of income and pride to the community. The army, with its constant demand for short-cropped hair, became the business' best client. Then the project had to close up shop after threats from the guerrillas. Even the act of cutting hair had become politicized, trapped between two armed actors.

I keep scribbling in my notebook. Community organizers. Industrial sewing workshops. New agricultural techniques. Health brigades. Peace laboratories. Literacy and postliteracy courses.

School restaurants. Promoting employment and sustainable development. There are strings and strings of words, hopeful projects, spots of light and optimism.

Among my scribbles is a statement from Cordepaz, a development group that is working in the eastern plains of Colombia: "La prevalencia del conflicto ha movilizado a amplias capas de la sociedad civil organizada alrededor de distintas iniciativas y organizaciones en busca de generar acciones colectivas que permitan prevenir y contener el conflicto, promover una cultura de reconciliación y perdón en los niveles locales y regionales, generar acciones que favorezcan a los grupos más afectados, mejorar las condiciones materiales y de bienestar para los grupos mas pobres de población, atención de población desplazada y muchas más." (The prevalence of the conflict has mobilized ample sectors of civil society organized around different initiatives and organizations to seek to generate collective actions that allow for the prevention and containment of the conflict, to promote a culture of reconciliation and forgiveness on local and regional levels, to generate actions that favor the most affected groups, to improve the material conditions and well-being of the poorest sectors of the society, attention to war refugees and much more.)

The language feels a bit academic, kind of the language that I like to edit into more accessible journalistic terms for *ReVista*, the magazine I edit at Harvard. But right now I'm just thankful for the words.

The words bring together the complicated goals and challenges as Colombia struggles to strengthen its civil society and put an end to its decades-long violence. The words summarize a Colombia in which it will be safe to cut hair.

And the challenge of reconstructing a society in which a community activist cannot finish her presentation without remembering the time the river ran red.

Dogs

Mangy dogs used to roam the downtown streets of Bogotá in menacing packs. The thin, hungry, flea-infested dogs rummaged through pestilent garbage and lapped up water in the gracious Rebecca fountain near the city's most elegant hotel at the time. They roamed alone and they roamed with the city's street urchins, as hungry and thin as the dogs. They left their excrement on the streets and growled at anyone who showed the least sign of fear. That usually included me.

When I came to Bogotá in 1975, the street dogs were an inevitable, depressing, and threatening part of the cityscape. And although I'd visited the city many times since then, I only noticed the absence of the dogs when I returned for my Fulbright sabbatical year in Bogotá.

One morning, leaving my downtown apartment early for a workshop, I saw a half-asleep unshaven homeless man in little more than rags huddled into a torn cardboard box on my street corner. He was surrounded by mattress stuffing and torn cloth; next to him was a blond and rather dirty dog, echoing the shape of his body, sharing body heat. There was a sense of belonging, man and dog.

It was only then that I remembered the packs of dogs. Even when they roamed with street urchins, they never seemed to belong to each other. And they were everywhere.

I began to look for the street dogs on my usual routes, which span a large section of the city. There were none in the downtown area, and none in the Chapinero shopping area, none in the elegant part of town, and none near the universities and theatres. I looked for the dogs near the open-air markets, where it seemed that street dogs ought to roam. Once in a while, I saw a scruffy dog that looked as if it might be abandoned or perhaps just looking for its equally poor owner. The packs of dogs seemed to have disappeared.

Instead, I see Dobermans and Rottweilers and pit bull terriers with muzzles covering their faces and with cloth flaps on their sides announcing the names of their security companies. Security dogs check cars for bombs at supermarket garages and hotels. They walk slowly and stately around the cars, sniffing and smelling, and then return to their positions, accompanying security guards, waiting for the next car. They are part of the landscape. One doesn't think about their presence: these antibomb and antidrug dogs are just a silent part of what President Uribe calls "democratic security." As a matter of fact, I've never heard one bark.

I continue to look for the street dogs. Instead, I see dog walkers. In the tree-lined La Castellana neighborhood, a long-haired man in his early thirties pumps his bicycle slowly, holding the leashes of poodles and Dalmatians and German shepherds trotting behind him. In the colonial Candelaria, an elderly man with a scruffy beard walks along with ten or so well-bred dogs, presumably not all of them his. Most of the dog walkers are in the elegant part of town, the northern stretch, but I see dog walkers in the parks around downtown and even on the sidewalks, where the street dogs used to roam.

I think of the homeless man with his dog. Perhaps what has changed most in this city is a sense of belonging. People no longer throw garbage on the streets; they don't push and shove while waiting for a bus; and they consider themselves "citizens" of this sprawling city, even if they come from elsewhere. I've always loved this city and always felt a sense of belonging here, but I often felt in the minority. Not now. People are proud of the Trans-Milenio that unites the city with its fast and modern buses, proud of the libraries and parks, the museums and open-air festivals. Perhaps this is no longer a place for stray dogs.

In October, just two months into my stay, a bomb shattered the vehicle of Senator Germán Vargas Lleras. The senator escaped unharmed, but Lucas, a mutt belonging to Luis Antonio

Molina Ruiz, a homeless man, was killed. The newspaper carried a front-page photo of the man embracing the cadaver of his lost pet.

TransMilenio

I was speeding past the traffic jams. Shiny Mercedes, crowded Renaults, and an occasional battered Chevy waited bumper-to-bumper on the Autopista, the northern highway that is the gateway to Bogotá.

It wasn't the first time I'd taken the TransMilenio rapid bus service, and it certainly won't be the last. However, I'd decided to mount the buses one sunny Saturday in the urban equivalent of a cheap joy ride (1,200 pesos, or around 50 cents) to explore the system from one end to the other.

I've chosen a blue seat and feel slightly guilty about it. Blue seats are reserved for the handicapped, the pregnant, those with small children, and the elderly. My image of myself in Bogotá is often of the twenty-eight-year-old journalist who fell in love with this chaotic city, its green spaces and bookstores. It's thirty-one years later, and if someone wants to challenge that I'm elderly enough to sit in a blue seat, I can always point to the gray streaks in my auburn hair. No one challenges me.

A woman in her twenties with a heavy bag does plop herself down next to me, and I wonder about the sanctity of the blue seats. A nun boards the TransMilenio, a middle-aged woman with a peaceful face. The young woman springs up and offers her blue seat to the sister. A man sitting nearby offers to carry the woman's heavy bag in his lap, although he doesn't offer her his seat. There's an unofficial sense of order and kindness here, but no one's enforcing it. It just happens, a spontaneous culture of citizenry.

The sleek red bus is modernistic, and the bus stations look like something out of fantasized space community. Huge elevated walkways connect the stations with sidewalks. The TransMilenio is the pride and joy of Bogotá. It makes people want to belong to the city, no matter from whence they come.

I've taken my Saturday exploratory bus tour to look out of the window and see how city space has changed. And yet I am constantly drawn in by the way citizen behavior has also changed. I remember sitting on a *buseta*, a microbus, some twenty-five years ago. I had just come back from a trip to sea level and was feeling on the verge of an asthma attack in Bogotá's high altitude. A gentleman in a suit was puffing away on an unfiltered cigarette; I felt as if I were being strangled by the smoke. I decided to approach him politely and said, "Sir, excuse me, but I'm slightly asthmatic and feeling sick, and I'd really appreciate it if you would put out your cigarette." He looked at me with a rude stare. "If it's bothering you, get off the bus," he snapped. "I have the right to smoke."

How far away that seems from this high, spacious bus where no one is smoking and no one is eating, where music is not blaring and only an occasional lurch is felt at a stoplight. No brakes squeal and no fumes belch; all TransMilenio buses run on diesel in compliance with Euro II emission standards. Both a mechanical voice and a moving electronic sign announce the next stop, and passengers form lines to enter the bus in an orderly fashion.

The city has expanded, but the new bus system has reduced commuting time for many. When I lived in Bogotá for *la primera ronda*, the city just about ended at Unicentro, the city's first mall, built the year after I came. Going south, it ended in Ciudad Kennedy, a working-class community named after the U.S. president. Now it extends north and west and south for miles and miles and miles and then climbs up the mountains, in some areas with elegant high-rises and in others, with *barrios de invasión*, mountainside squatter communities. On the TransMilenio, I transverse the city from its northernmost tip to the far south in less than an hour. I stick to the red buses, the main lines. If I wanted to go further, I could board the green feeder buses that go into the poorest communities, skirting rocks on unpaved streets and competing with bikes and dogs for public space.

The system started in December 2000 and now carries more than a million passengers daily on a fifty-mile network. Trans-Milenio's buses operate on central lanes of existing streets, segregated from the general traffic, with stations located every few city blocks on their designated lines. The city master plan envisions a 241-mile network of trunk corridors and supporting feeder routes that would transport about five million passengers daily. The system is the centerpiece for long-term urban renewal, including a strategy that emphasizes walking and cycling and discourages private vehicle use.

I look out the window at the traffic jams of impatient drivers waiting to get to the sprawling shopping centers of the north, and think of how much more there is to do.

Pollution from cars and the old buses shrouds the city, much of it trapped by the surrounding mountains. The city's population has boomed—more than 140,000 people move to Bogotá each year. About half of them migrate from the countryside, many fleeing Colombia's internal war. Rising incomes and sharply decreased import taxes have led to more cars and more gridlock. More than 70,000 new cars hit the roads every year. Indeed, a plate restriction system in which cars with certain license plates cannot be on the road in peak hours has encouraged some families to invest in two cars to have an alternate. But the TransMilenio is a jewel that saves citizens an average of three hundred hours of commuting time annually.

I tell myself to stop thinking and to start concentrating on the view out of the window. Reaching the end of the line, I switch to another going southward. I observe blocks and blocks of similar stores grouped together. I've always wondered about this Bogotá phenomenon: blocks and blocks of hardware stores, then blocks and blocks of pet stores, blocks of institutes for technical learning, and then blocks of stores selling motorcycle helmets. The speed of the TransMilenio gives me a feeling of the city that is much more encompassing than riding the slower buses or just strolling.

I travel past the San Andresitos, sprawling markets of contraband and semicontraband that dates back to when imports were prohibitively expensive, past the old-fashioned railroad station that now houses a tourist train, past dozens and dozens of outlet stores, and now on toward the poorer south of the city.

The colors of the city turn from blues and greens and oranges to brick reds and gray. The houses often seem half-finished, layers and layers of brick with laundry floating on lines at the top. The side streets are unpaved. Bicycles are everywhere, and the traffic jams have ceased. I spot an open-air market with mangos and bananas and leafy green vegetables. We pass the stop for the Tintal Library, a gleaming new public facility in the heart of this rundown district. Many young people—probably students—get off at this stop. The prosperous north is still divided from the poorer south, but projects like the TransMilenio and public libraries are bringing the two areas closer together.

I hear accents from all over the country on the TransMilenio, the singsong of the south and the wide vowels of the coastal areas. I see citizens of Afro-Colombian and indigenous descent, and every shade in between. I change buses and travel in another direction, watching the folks line up for the green feeder buses to their neighborhoods, distant places that often did not have the benefit of public transportation before.

I admire the politeness and the sense of orderly belonging. The city belongs to everyone, even to those who were not born here. That's an attitude I know from New York, but it's new here. And I feel a happy surge of hope for this country, this city, that I love so much.

I used to hate the three tall towers that thrust against the verdant mountains.

I used to think that the red brick towers dug into the landscape, belonging to some other city and some other space, created a scar of modernity.

That was thirty years ago. I don't think my taste in architecture has changed that much, but my relationship to the Torres del Parque certainly has.

For one thing, I can now see the towers from my wide windows across the Parque de la Independencia. They do not invade the green view; they blend with it. Perhaps the brick has faded over the years, or more likely is that Bogotá is now a city of apartment buildings. My friends grew up in houses; their children are being raised in elevator buildings with doormen.

The few times that I went to the Torres in the mid-1970s and 1980s, I approached the buildings in a taxi, riding up in the elevator to play Scrabble with a friend. The view from his apartment was of the bullring and had me thinking that the towers weren't all that bad from inside. Yet I still disliked them.

Now I live in a historical 1962 building called the Embajador right on the Séptima and gaze up at the towers. Lots of friends live there; the avenue up from the Torres has become a gastronomic paradise, with Mexican, Arab, Cuban, *costeño* (Colombian coastal food), and even a gringo restaurant called the Hamburguesería; my dry cleaner is in the Torres complex, and so is a fragrant bakery with excellent *tinto*—the Colombian equivalent of espresso. A coffeehouse-bookstore is right across the street, and so is a video place that rents art films. Needless to say, I walk frequently up through the Parque de la Independencia and wend my way through the Torres to this Bogotá version of Greenwich Village.

The steep red brick steps still manage to take the wind out of me. But I often encounter friends with their babies and acquaintances with dogs. I see students and children and old people that seem to have an easier time with the steps than I do, and sometimes I don't see anyone I know, but lots of people with a vaguely intellectual air that look as if I should know them.

When I look out of my window, I also see the Museum of Modern Art, a squat red brick building that is at once friendly and ugly. After arriving in August, I soon learned Rogelio Salmona was the architect of both the museum and the towers.

I should have guessed that because of his signature use of red brick, but then again Bogotá is filled with red brick. So when the museum hosted an exhibit of Salmona's work, I went in spite of my fairly low expectations: probably lots of photos and architectural mock-ups.

Children and their parents were ducking under some huge Japanese-like lampshades. Each revolving lampshade bore the name of a Salmona project. I held my breath and ducked. I found myself inside a familiar landscape, the steps leading up to the towers, a space with dogs and kids and folks with shopping bags, a community space. It was no accident that I had hated the towers before and now enjoyed them as a social space. Salmona had conceived them not just to be glimpsed from a distance but to be experienced.

The Salmona exhibit was the most interactive I've seen in Colombia. Children sprawled on the floor, drawing copies of the building. A teenager was reading an essay on architecture to a group of classmates. Museumgoers watched Salmona explain his architecture on a flat digital television screen, and films flashed overhead. There were indeed the photos and the architectural mock-ups I had expected, but the explanations gave them context.

I paused in front of one explanatory sign: "Rogelio Salmona's innovative proposals seek to construct a more democratic city, providing public spaces for living together that give incentives to sociability, mutual recognition, and social organization."

Salmona's work, influenced by French architect Le Corbusier, was a response to the migration to Bogotá in the 1950s, I learned from one of the signs. His buildings—many of them so-called social housing—sought to confront marginality, unemployment, and housing shortages. Whether public or private, for the rich or the poor, his buildings were surrounded by trees and parks and walkways. Written explanations informed me that some of the parks that Salmona had designed for social housing were never built. None of the signs explained what I remember from Colombian history: heavy migration to Bogotá was caused by people fleeing from La Violencia, the bloody war between Liberals and Conservatives that wracked Colombia's countryside. At home, I'm reading a book of journalistic reminiscences by Carlos Villar Borda. Just last night, I was reading his description of the *cortes*, the intricate machete slashes used by one political band against the other, about the way fetuses were carved out of mother's wombs and replaced with the head of a cow.

This is what the rural population was fleeing, and this is the city that Salmona wanted to construct to combat those memories. And here I stumble on another sign: "The architecturally designed building is a place of encounter, to love and to rest, to discover and to experience the passing of time."

I had come to the exhibit to learn a bit more about my neighboring buildings. I had come to the exhibit perhaps to take a break from thinking about journalism and journalism education and elections and wars and nightmares. And even though the word "violence" was never once mentioned in the exhibit, what I had found was an antidote to violence, the creation of public space and a communal identity.

The kids were still sprawled on the floor, drawing buildings and coloring them, as I left the museum. I glanced up. There were the towers, strong and stable against the glowing mountains.

I love the three tall towers.

I confess. I have a love-hate relationship with living downtown, in el centro. When I walk out my front door, I am frequently faced with homeless people and the constant reminder of Colombia's oft-invisible war: the displaced, *los desplazados.*

I never give money, although I often buy bread and sometimes even milk and fruit for the displaced. They sit on the sidewalk, on cardboard or the cold cement, and prop up signs that say "desplazados" or "somos víctimas de la violencia" (we are victims of the violence). Many have children with them. Some are neatly dressed in once-fine clothes that have seen better days, and others wear tatters. Some are con artists, and some even are said to rent the children that surround them to get better donations.

I first saw Carlos Alberto carrying his nine-year-old daughter Marilyn piggyback right at the corner of my apartment building. I didn't know their names then. I was struck by his strong black features and by Marilyn's tidy braids and thought that perhaps they had been visiting my neighbor Piedad Córdoba, a black congresswoman. I noticed that Carlos Alberto's right hand was bandaged with white gauze.

In my journalism workshops here, I teach my students to listen to the invisible people around them, the watchmen, the maids, the street people. Yet often I am timid myself about approaching the people on the street, especially if I don't have a reporter's protective notebook. After all, I live on the corner. It could be dangerous, I rationalize.

Yet I was pulled in by Marilyn's friendly, curious gaze. I asked a vague question, like whether they lived nearby. Carlos Alberto also had one of those cardboard signs with him, but it was hidden from sight as he boosted his daughter onto his shoulders. I spotted it only when we began to talk. The story came spilling out in bits and pieces.

He had a small fishing business in Barbacoas, and the paramilitary members kept coming by for a *vacuna* (payment of protection money), and the quantity kept on increasing until he protested. His little boats were burned, and he was held and tortured, he told me. He fled with his family to nearby Pasto, in the south of the country, and was then sent to Cali, further north. A refugee organization in Cali told him that he would receive swifter help in Bogotá, so he came with his eldest daughter. His wife and other four children would follow.

He said he'd been trying to get help for three weeks now and hadn't been able to find a job. His voice mounted slightly with bitterness. "When tourists come to Barbacoas, we treat them like kings; we show them around; we share our food," he complained. "Here we are treated like dirt. They treat my little girl that way too."

Carlos Alberto waxed eloquent; I wished that I had a tape recorder or could take notes without causing suspicions. "This is an illogical war," he asserted. "I can't even pronounce that word well," sliding over the syllables of *ilógico*. "This war makes no sense. It's all about drugs and power."

I could see him as a community leader, as a small businessman, as a person filled with pride, and yet I felt his frustration and bitterness. He insisted on peeling off the gauze bandage, so I could see the nearly healed knife marks. "It's not ugly anymore," he reassured me, "but it still hurts."

He was trying to get Marilyn into a public school, he said. I asked her if she liked Bogotá. She answered with one word, almost without intonation: "No." Carlos Alberto wanted to keep talking. We sat on the steps of a nearby office building. He never asked me for money and was too absorbed in the conversation to actively panhandle anyone else. A young office worker noticed his almost hidden sign and swiftly thrust 2,000 pesos (just under US$1) into his hand and moved on rapidly. I decided it was time to get going. I felt that Carlos Alberto wanted to keep talking, but he reassured me that he and Marilyn always came to my street corner. We would see each other soon.

For me, Carlos Alberto and Marilyn have names now. But every day, I stroll by other displaced people and exchange at most only a greeting, retreating to the comfort of urban anonymity.

The United Nations High Commission for Refugees (UNHCR) recently issued a report finding that Colombia has the largest quantity of displaced people in the Western Hemisphere, and the second highest in the world after Sudan. In 2004, Colombia's Constitutional Court declared that the displaced population here represents an "estado de cosas inconstitucional" (an unconstitutional state of affairs) and ordered that the government make the necessary budgetary effort to cope with the problem. The government assigned millions of pesos to the effort—but still far short of what is needed.

No one has an exact figure about the number of displaced people in Colombia. The Colombian government says there are 1.7 million (since 1995); the United Nation counts between 2 and 3 million (since 1986); the Consultancy on Human Rights and Displacement (CODHES), a Colombian nongovernmental organization, estimates 3.7 million (since 1985); and the Colombian Bishops' Conference, together with the Universidad de los Andes, counts 2.5 million people.

A poll by the Colombian Bishops' Conference and the Universidad de los Andes found that 76 percent of displaced people in Colombia considered that their personal finances were much worse off or somewhat worse than before they had fled their homes because of the war. More than half the families had owned property before the events that caused them to flee, the poll found, and 46 percent had owned their own homes.

I read a report by the Norwegian Refugee Council/Global IDP (Internal Displaced People) Project on Colombia. Just glancing through the table of contents is mind-boggling: "Agents of Displacement: Paramilitary Groups; Agents of Displacement: Guerrilla Groups; Agents of Displacement: Displacements Caused by Fumigations and Plan Colombia; Displacement Induced by Drug Trafficking; Displacement Rooted in Territorial and Resource Interests."

I think of Carlos Alberto and his "illogical war." I search for him and Marilyn on the Séptima; I look for them on my street corner. I see other displaced people and other signs and other children and other lives. The father and daughter may have found help, or they may have given up. I probably will never know. Carlos Alberto and Marilyn have been swallowed up into the metropolis.

Time

I spotted the middle-aged woman with her most-likely-dyed blond hair in the window of a bus as the vehicle waited for the traffic light to change. Her fingers were caught in an upward dance as she applied mascara to her lashes and then began to outline her lips with a gloss just as the bus took off. I watched her as the vehicle lurched. Her hand held steady. The bus disappeared from sight.

It was the first time I had seen such a pantomime in Bogotá. It certainly wasn't the last. Women spread out their cosmetics on their laps as they travel on buses, *busetas*, or the TransMilenio, a sign of time starvation. They must perform these cosmetic routines in spaces of transition, in travel time between home and office, or office and night school. I imagine children at home, groping at their mother's skirts (or more often, pants) before she leaves for work. I imagine the last minutes spent on an algebra lesson before running out the door. Time is always short in today's Bogotá.

When I came to Bogotá in 1975, practically every store in the city shut down between noon and 2 p.m. Banks and government offices closed; so did bookstores and galleries and other forms of entertainment. Workers went home for lunch, and the city sprang back to life after two—or sometimes three—hours.

As a newly arrived gringa, I found this immensely frustrating. I couldn't understand how anyone could spend two hours eating lunch. It was impossible to run errands. I dreamt of a movie theatre that would open at noon so that I could lose myself in the world of film. I ended up reading the newspaper and then taking a stroll to my post office box at Avianca—which was open for *jornada continua*, without a lunch break—to pick up my mail.

During the nine years I lived here back then, the city expanded northward and traffic jams kept many from going home for lunch. Lunch was still two hours, but now office workers ate in cafeterias and construction workers lunched out of wide-capped thermos bottles as they sat on the sidewalk and then played soccer. Gradually, offices and stores began to open at midday.

Yet there was always time. People stopped by each other's homes, and there always seemed to be time to chat. Meals were made from scratch, often by a maid, and takeout was unheard of.

Back in Bogotá for my Fulbright year, I often complain that I don't see my friends because they are too busy. My Christmas visits had given me a warped sense of time in Bogotá because people would drop what they were doing to make time to see me. I reminisce about the days when my dream was about a noontime movie and friends had time. (I was usually the guilty party, running off to cover some story or other.) The concept of time in Bogotá has metamorphosed into a fast-paced routine.

Some friends from Harvard point out that my friends don't have time because they are directors of institutes and museums and intellectual and journalistic leaders. That's true, but I always bring up the women on the bus. I hear a maid in the elevator complaining she doesn't have time to do her errands. At the flea market, I ask around for the organizer of some walking tours I've heard about, and when I ask the vendor who tells me about them whether he has tried out these forays, he replies, "I don't have time."

The television advertises pre-chopped onions, tomatoes, and cilantro, conveniently packaged to save you time. Fast food—whether it's hamburgers or pizza or traditional Colombian fare like empanadas—has become popular. So has home delivery. Office workers eat lunch at their desks.

Even Sundays—the sacrosanct day of leisure and family time—are now under attack. The Bogotá chapter of Fenalco, the National Merchants Federation, found that Sunday was the second most popular day of the week on which to shop (Saturday remains the most popular). Indeed, one out of every five families in Bogotá—with a slight drop in the category of high-income families—squeeze their shopping into Sunday.

This Sunday shopping and periodic late-night shopping, called Bogotá Despierta, do generate a festive air, with multigenerational families parading through the mall to enjoy ice cream cones and window shopping, as well as to run essential errands. However, it's still an erosion—or perhaps a metamorphosis—of leisure time. In Bogotá, according to a McCann Erickson poll earlier this year, only three out of ten city residents consider free time important.

I now go shopping at midnight myself, since many supermarkets are open twenty-four hours a day. So are some fast-food restaurants and drugstores. Transportation time in this increasingly sprawling city cuts into productive time. Fewer maids and less other domestic support mean extra duties, particularly for women.

The TransMilenio bus system has electronic signs that tell riders exactly how many minutes before their bus arrives. I've seen those kind of signs in Germany, but not even in the States. This is no longer the land of mañana.

The shift is not in my imagination. According to a 2006 report by the International Labour Organization, Colombians work harder than anyone else, except for South Koreans, in terms of hours: 2,236 hours yearly, compared to 1,200 hours yearly in Holland. The South Koreans beat out the Colombians with 2,400 hours yearly.

There has always been a strong work ethic in Antioquia, the region where Medellín is located. Perhaps Colombian president Álvaro Uribe is helping to popularize that region's work obsession throughout the country with his much publicized lack of sleep.

But it used to be that people—some friends from Medellín included—would boast about stretching a three-day weekend into four or five days. I remember that it was nearly impossible to find office workers at their jobs, particularly in government posts, after lunch on a Friday afternoon. That was called *viernes cultural*—cultural Friday—and it was a part of the rhythm of the week.

As I think about culture (even though the term was generally a euphemism for drinking), I remember to check this week's movie listings. My eye catches the listing for the Ópera Plaza, a movie house near my apartment. There is a 1 p.m. movie, and next to the listing, in English, is the word "lunch."

The Story of the Weeping Camel is playing, and I decide to try out the lunch offer. For 6,000 pesos (around US$2.50), I get to see the movie, eat a ham sandwich, drink a bottle of soda pop, and munch on popcorn. The concession stand operator brings me the lunch on a tray. The theatre is nowhere near full, but the sound of munching popcorn and bottle opening distracts me as I watch the camels.

The movie is over at 2:45, and I walk out with my fellow spectators to a drizzly Bogotá afternoon. I have just fulfilled my long-ago wish of watching a movie at noontime, and fleetingly think that one should be careful what one wishes for. But then again, it was still a two-hour lunch.

Plaza de Bolívar

The oversized blue angels with their yellow wings hover over the Plaza de Bolívar. It is Christmastime in Bogotá.

An angel reflects in glass doors leading to the colonial-style chapel of the cathedral, filling it with an image of peace. Shafts of light illuminate the angels.

I always think of the Plaza de Bolívar as colonial, but in truth, only the Capilla del Sagrario dates back to the seventeenth century. The cathedral is neoclassical, constructed in the nineteenth century after building disasters and earthquakes. The Palacio de Justicia on the other corner was rebuilt after the army staged a fierce offensive in a tragic and brutal attempt to reclaim the seat of the Supreme Court, taken over by M-19 guerrillas in 1985. The rest of the buildings, or so my Lonely Planet handbook tells me, were finished in the twentieth century.

A hefty Santa Claus waits in a flower-lined horse-drawn carriage for clients to drive around the plaza area. An excited toddler, practically dragging his father and mother, approaches. Shoppers with packages, families of tourists, lawyers with briefcases, and office workers are feeding the pigeons with leftover bread and packages of popcorn. Couples stroll hand in hand. I notice a large group of people looking at something over by the Congressional Building. I have some spare time before meeting some friends from out of town at the restaurant next to the nearby opera house, so I wander over.

White-painted bricks have been placed in a solemn grid in front of the Congress. Rustic red peers out from underneath, and over each brick is pasted a name. Most carry a date of birth and a date of death. I try to count the bricks, but the crowd gets in the way. Dozens and dozens of bricks, maybe three hundred, maybe more. I look at the dates. These were young men and women who mostly died young, victims of violence. White and pink carnations are strewn over the memorial. A middle-aged man with a briefcase points out that some of the bricks are dedicated to those who disappeared during the conflagration of the Palace of Justice, workers who had supposedly been conducted to safety and were never seen again. The crowd is mostly silent, the silence of a cemetery. The angels of peace watch over the scene, but it is the shadow of violence that permeates the scene.

I have been in Bogotá for almost four months now. Christmas is one of my favorite times of year here. The city slows down. Friends visit. Nine days of communal prayer, singing, and festivities—*la novena*—mark the entry into the Christmas celebration. This year I attend five *novenas*: one is very prayerful, with tones of mysticism and colonial song; another is joyful, with lots of *aguardiente* (an anise-flavored firewater) and food from several regions of the country; a third revolves around children, emphasizing song and lots of traditional musical instruments. The other two *novenas* fall somewhere in between, but I am struck that no one mentions war and no one mentions peace.

Violence, especially in the later years, formed the backdrop of my nine years in Colombia in the 1970s and 1980s. In the terrible short visit in which I returned to collect my belongings to move to Managua in April 1984, I remember Javier Baena of the Associated Press sweeping alongside me in his car and crying out, "Rodrigo Lara has just been gunned down." The thirty-seven-year-old justice minister was murdered by a man on a red motorcycle because of the government official's war on drug trafficking.

As I look at the white carnations among the memorial bricks, I think how urban violence and political conflict had a constant and defined presence during those years. *Gamines*—small and violent street children—ripped earrings off of women as they walked along the Séptima; men on motorcycles gunned down political figures; bombs went off; and embassies were taken over. Even then violence was far from the whole story. It erupted; it confronted, like a force of nature. And the rest of the time there were sunsets and bookstores and movies and social projects.

Now it feels as if the war is always somewhere else. I watch it on the evening news; I see it in the eyes of the displaced people who beg for food along the streets; it is the subject of forums, academic studies, and human rights reports. Am I getting a distorted view from Bogotá, where a series of excellent mayors have improved infrastructure and quality of life? Or has the war become invisible and insidious? I feel that I understand less than when I left Cambridge four months before.

In any case, my friends who are coming to visit will be excellent interlocutors. I can ask them my questions. They live in Bucaramanga, ten hours north of Bogotá.

We meet at a rooftop hotel restaurant with a view of church spires and red-tiled roofs below. The meal is excellent, and we chat about the past and plans for the future. I have known these friends for nearly thirty years, and we have intermittently kept in touch.

I ask them about life in Bucaramanga. They tell me about possible job contracts and cultural events. I press them. What about the war? What about violence? Do you feel it?

My friend, whom I'll call Patricia here to protect her privacy, said no, explaining that they live in a safe part of the city in a nice apartment. It is calm in Bucaramanga now, she tells me, and even the roads around the city are fairly safe.

We go on to some other subject and finally wander out into the starlit night. We keep talking and begin to walk past the Plaza de Bolívar. Santa Claus has gone home for the night, but I notice that candles are still flickering on the other side of the plaza, joining the carnations around the memorial bricks. "Come see something interesting," I say enthusiastically to my friends.

Patricia gazes at the candles and begins to cry, tears flowing silently. I look at her with a sympathetic question mark in my eyes. It is then that she tells me that she has lost two brothers to the violence. One, her youngest brother, was shot and killed when he was riding in a car with two of his friends. It might have been a case of mistaken identity. Or it may have been only that he had committed the crime of being young.

The other brother was killed by the guerrillas on his *finca* (property). She doesn't know why.

Patricia had lost two brothers to both sides of the war. I don't ask her how long ago the murders happened. I don't ask her if she and her family had sought justice. We just stand in the plaza and gaze at the candles, silent witnesses to the invisible wounds.

The horse clops along a wide Bogotá avenue, dragging along a planklike cart laden with cardboard and other materials to be recycled. The driver of the horse-drawn cart concentrates on the animal, ignoring the trendy shopping centers and fashionable outdoor cafés. The horse mixes with polluting buses and Mercedes-Benzes and motorcycles. Just a block away a sleek Trans-Milenio bus speeds along.

This horse isn't an aberration. Bogotá has an estimated eleven thousand of these horse-drawn vehicles. The drivers are called *zorreros*, and most of them make their living by recycling garbage. The city government estimates that each person in the prosperous north of Bogotá, where this horse is working, produces a kilo of garbage daily, while residents of the poorer barrios produce a mere 0.45 kilo (about a pound).

These aren't Bogotá's only horses. Mounted policemen on sleek, shiny horses attend sports events and concerts; flower-lined horse-drawn carriages drive tourists around at the Plaza de Bolívar.

Animals are part of the scenery of daily life. As I leave a Jesuit research center near a prestigious private school, I spot a rooster on the sidewalk. He just stands there, part of the scenery. School-children walk past him without noticing. Just a few blocks away, the tallest Bogotá skyscrapers spiral into the sky.

I hesitate to write about the animals, even if they do fascinate me. When I was learning German in Berlin, a fellow student, a young Turkish man married to a German woman, was highly offended when I said something about camels in Istanbul. Animals certainly aren't the only story here, but their ubiquitous presence in urban life shows a strong link to the rural past and country values.

Horses and burros can be seen from the classrooms of the National University. Cows wander through the lawns and pastures of the sprawling campus, a few minutes from downtown Bogotá. There are fewer than a year ago after an episode of *aftosa*, hoof-and-mouth disease, but the students say the bovine population is once again growing. A February 4 (2006) article in *El Tiempo* tells me that there are 3,770 cows in Bogotá. They mostly graze on vacant grassy lots on the outskirts of the city; I've seen them on the way out to the countryside on weekends. The news item also relates that the city of Bogotá and the municipality of Zipaquirá, about an hour away, have signed an agreement. The cows are leaving the city and going to graze—hopefully—in greener pastures. The university's urban cows, a cross between bovine lawnmowers and teacher's pets, will most likely remain.

I haven't seen a follow-up article in the paper about the wayward cows, so I decide to resort to Google to see if I can find the information. A search for the word *vacas* produces a lot of references to sacred cows and cow's milk, but only the original article. I decide to browse for "animals."

Rats are being trained to detect land mines in Colombia—mines that have caused the deaths of 476 children in the past sixteen years. The rats have names like "Lola," "Lucrecia," "Luna," and "Espejo." In Pereira an elephant—originally from the hacienda of drug lord Pablo Escobar—killed a veterinarian from Bogotá in the local zoo. Thoroughbred horses and dogs are offered to clients all over the country and even the world.

But I can't find any more references to cows. I am struck by several Internet references to the *zorreros*, though, and decide to investigate further. I discovered a 2003 Constitutional Court decision that gave me new respect for the often aging horses that clop along Bogotá streets, or perhaps I should say respect for the way law and democracy can sometimes work in Colombia.

In 2002 a law was passed to "eradicate" animal-drawn vehicles, with the exception of tourist carriages, within a year. But a group of *zorreros* brought a *tutela* to the Constitutional Court, appealing the law. *Tutelas* are the common man's (or woman's) lawsuits, defending citizens' rights. The 1991 Constitution, a sweeping and egalitarian reform of Colombian law—at least on paper—allows citizens to request immediate court action if they feel that their constitutional rights are being violated and if there is no other legal recourse.

This is precisely what the *zorreros* did. They filed a *tutela* under the auspices of the Asociación de Carreteros de Bogotá to assert that their right to freedom and their right to job stability were being affected by the law.

The highly legalistic language in the suit argues that the state cannot restrict liberty, unless the intention is to protect third parties or the established legal order, and that the horses and their carts did not do so.

Reading the case, I was sure that the *zorreros* were going to lose. The Animal Defense League testified against them, saying that the old horses were mistreated and then sold for horse meat. The Ministry of Transport asserted that the state has the obligation of ensuring the security and comfort of its inhabitants and, in particular, pedestrians and handicapped people, indirectly alleging that the vehicles were a public nuisance. Besides, recycling can be done without horses, so the right to work was not really affected, and the 2002 law made a provision for job retraining.

Much to my surprise, the court found in favor of the *zorreros*, saying that the legislative decision to eradicate the horse-drawn vehicles was unconstitutional because it represented an imminent violation of the right to work of the operators of animal-drawn vehicles. It was fine to offer retraining opportunities, but the measure could be reconsidered only when effective job opportunities were put into place in actuality, not in theory.

The court cited Article 13 of the 1991 Constitution: "The State will promote conditions so that equality will be real and effective and will adopt measures in favor of groups that are discriminated against or marginalized," as well as protecting "especially those persons who for economic reasons . . . find themselves in circumstances of manifest weakness."

The weak had won out for once. Now, whenever I see a horse clopping along the street, I think not so much of Bogotá's rural roots, but in the small victory for an urban and democratic future.

But I still don't know what is happening with the cows.

El Chocó: Never to the Jungle

When I first came to Colombia in 1975, right before I started a job as Bogotá editor for the *Cali Chronicle*, I traveled around the country from the Andean mountains to the tropical coast and the eastern plains.

I had no plan and even less purpose. I carried a suitcase; I wasn't even a true backpacker, avoiding guidebooks and, for the most part, other gringos. In Cartagena, the tropical colonial city on the Atlantic coast, I met a young man named Mario with huge brown eyes, an earnest smile, and an immense curiosity about life. We sat on a park bench and talked for hours and hours. He was from the poor downtown area and was going to school at night.

When it came time to leave Cartagena, I asked Mario for advice on where to go next on my journey. I was thinking about two alternatives. One was the Chocó, a steamy jungle on Colombia's Pacific coast, populated by Afro-descendants. The other was Caracas, the capital of Venezuela, a booming metropolis. "Caracas," said Mario, enthusiastically. "There's nothing to see in Chocó except monkeys and poverty."

I ended up going to neither, taking off to the coastal cities of Barranquilla and Santa Marta. A month later, I started my job in Bogotá.

As a newspaper editor and later a foreign correspondent in Bogotá, I mostly forgot about the Chocó. I met plenty of people from Medellín, the industrious textile city where I had started my Colombian journey. My best friend was from Barranquilla, on the Atlantic coast, a lawyer who had done her studies in Bogotá and stayed. At handicrafts stores, public festivals, and even music stores, I was reminded of other far-flung places in the jungles and plains of Colombia. Chocó was not seen or heard of, or as they say in literature classes back at Harvard, it was not part of the public imaginary. And I still have never been there.

I now peruse the Lonely Planet guide to Colombia to see if I can find a generic description of the Chocó region. I am surprised to see that the region is not in the index, at least not in the edition I own. Neither is Quibdó, the departmental capital. I finally discover a reference to Chocó under northwestern Colombia, where I find what I know already, that Chocó is one of Colombia's poorest and least developed regions. Lonely Planet doesn't cover the region, citing security problems with guerrillas and paramilitaries, as well as lack of road infrastructure.

This lack of infrastructure is what kept me from the region later in the 1970s when I met a young gringa jewelry maker who lived in a beach area of the Chocó. I think Meredith might have been in the Peace Corps at one point, or just a friend of Peace Corps workers I met in Bogotá. We exchanged carrot cake recipes and general talk on life, and she invited me to come visit her whenever I wanted. I decided to take her up on her offer, so she sent me directions. First a bus or plane to Quibdó, then a boat on the river for almost a day, and then I had to hire a mule. It was the mule that did me in psychologically. I decided I would keep up my friendship with Meredith by mail or during her Bogotá visits.

I now understand that Mario—who by now had married a lovely woman from Medellín and built a small house in a working-class residential area of Cartagena—did not recommend Chocó because it represented underdevelopment, poverty, and isolation, the Colombia he wished to leave behind.

According to Colombian government statistics, almost one out of every two citizens of the Chocó lives below the poverty line. It is the only Colombian department that borders on two oceans. The Colombian Ministry of Economic Development's tourist guidebook—which unlike the Lonely Planet's does mention Chocó—tells me that the department depends on mining and lumbering as its main sources of income. The San Juan Valley in the Chocó is the world's richest region in platinum. And it adds that the name of Chocó derives from "the Indian community of the Chocoes, who share their territory with the predominant black community, which settled here after fleeing from slavery and violence."

In the thirty-one years since I first came to Colombia, Chocó continues to be poor and isolated. But now, instead of being a refuge from violence, it is an incubator for violence as fumigation displaces coca cultivation and drug traffic westward. Besides, the Chocó region has the asset of two ocean borders, making it attractive to drug traffickers seeking to move their merchandise northward.

The Diocese of Quibdó won the 2005 Colombian National Peace Prize, an award given yearly by a conglomeration of Colombian and international institutions. I didn't know that the church in Chocó was the winner when I showed up for the ceremony at the National Museum in Bogotá, a nineteenth-century prison, just a couple of months after I arrived in Bogotá for my Fulbright fellowship. The award was given for the "development of formative processes of human rights, cultural awareness, humanitarian assistance, and life plans." As it was further explained, "Always taking into account its commitment to life and in solidarity with the victims, the Diocese has taken up the voice of the people of Chocó to denounce and resist the violence along the Atrato River." Pastoral agents tended to 4,400 people through the extensive territory, much of it rural and inaccessible.

Father Albeiro Parra, director of the social pastoral department of the Diocese of Quibdó, declared in Spanish as he accepted the award: "On being awarded this prize, we have achieved one of our objectives: to make visible the difficult situation faced by the communities along the Atrato River in the Chocó. There we are witnesses to an armed conflict, a territorial dispute, and a resulting humanitarian crisis. Thus it is necessary for us to keep Chocó with a high degree of awareness on the national agenda."

In the back of the museum, a group of women community activists were selling handicrafts carved from seeds and wood. I bought a couple of necklaces. The crafts looked a bit familiar, and later I realized that I'd seen them at crafts fairs and Sunday markets in Bogotá without any mention of their origin.

Violence and lack of economic opportunities have led many rural denizens of the Chocó first to Quibdó and then on to Bogotá. They seek work as security guards and policemen. They open up fish restaurants with their special Pacific touches such as juices made of the fruit *borojó* that are supposed to have aphrodisiac powers. They bring with them their handicrafts and their music and their dance. They have transformed Bogotá from a white city to a salt-and-pepper metropolis.

My friends from the Universidad de los Andes like to go to the cavernous fish restaurants, often two-floor affairs with reasonable lunch prices, filled with office workers and students. The restaurants, with poetic names like "Sabores del Pacífico," are often decorated with murals: fishermen, palm trees, blue water, and ever bluer sky, a nostalgic and idealized rendering of home. They remind me of the murals that one often sees in Greek restaurants in New York, the homeland forgotten in space but translated into the aromas of home.

If I have never made it to the Chocó, the Chocó has come home to me in Bogotá.

Artists: Beyond the Invisible Door

The heavy wooden door has no sign. It is snuggled between an all-purpose drugstore and a dilapidated public telephone center, in front of a shoeshine stand. I pass the door almost everyday, since it is two blocks from my house along the crowded Séptima. I occasionally look up to the second floor of the buildings along the street and spot once-elegant wrought-iron balconies and ornate neoclassical trimmings typical of nineteenth-century republican architecture.

Today, as I stroll down the Séptima to buy bread and milk, I
notice that the "invisible" door is open, and a poster announces
that the building is one of the many sites of the Fortieth National
Salon of Artists. The sites are spread throughout the city, and I've
already been to an exhibit at the Colón Theatre that allowed me
to sit in the presidential first-tier box and hear recordings from
three different versions of Hamlet. At the National Library, I've
wandered through a multimedia exhibit on miners from the
Chocó region in the Pacific, listening to regional music and admiring the black-and-white photographs, noticing that a father
posing with his infant son in a nearly-Madonna pose was wearing
a Nike T-shirt.

The exhibits are all over the city, but I didn't realize there was
one behind the invisible door. The wood creaked as I walked in. A
security guard handed me a folder and told me the exhibit was on
both floors of the *casona*, an immense rambling house now used
by the Mapa Theatre group. I gazed at the high ceilings and the
intricate woodwork inspired by the ancient Greeks.

The house has good bones, but the stairs are rotting away
and most of the walls are unpainted. It would make a wonderful
haunted house, but for now, it's serving as an art gallery.

I am reminded of Miami Beach when I used to go there in
the early 1970s as a respite from my reporting job in Lakeland,
Florida. The rundown hotels cost $15 a night, and old folk from
the North sunned themselves on creaking porches. I only barely
noticed the architecture there, an ornate art deco that could be
glimpsed through the layers of paint. And now the ritzy beach
has capitalized on its architecture, carving the old-age homes
into classy hotels and fancy restaurants. What would the Séptima
look like if all its republican architecture were restored? if the
doors were no longer invisible?

Ironically, or perhaps intentionally, part of the exhibit is dedicated to utopian views of the city of Cali, a tropical city in Co lombia's southwest: "The chimerical city: utopian proposals for Cali." The exhibits don't quite seem to be connected, except that all the artists are from the Cali area.

A series of silent video clips lasting from one to three minutes focus on urban ennui. In one of them, a student pretends to die again and again, his body lined up against policelike chalk tracings on the street. The film captures people walking by, not noticing, or pretending not to notice.

There's also a series of paintings done as a sort of public performance, *How I See My City, How I Paint My City*, in which pedestrians picture their environment. I linger by another part of the exhibit on the human body, photographs, drawings, paintings, even a portrait done with baby's feces.

Finally, my eye catches what seems to be traditional Colombian embroidery on two cubed seats by a gallery window. I love embroidery, but for the most part the intricate handiwork I coveted when I lived here years ago has been replaced by machine-made Chinese imports. I come closer to the seats. The colors are bright and startling: blues, greens, yellows, reds, and oranges.

The figures in the embroidery become clear as I approach. One cubed seat is cartoonlike, with an outsized tank and two military figures that seem more like Spiderman than soldiers. Outlines of green embroidered trees and tall grass create a bucolic feel, but a thrusting orange streak spurts out from the tank. "Da-Bamn," reads the legend by the orange streak, just in case one didn't pick up the message from the visual cue.

On the adjacent seat, a bright yellow sun shines in the sky next to a puffy white cloud. Three green helicopters hover in the sky, which is white, not blue. On the ground are three dead soldiers in green-and-brown camouflage uniforms. A helmet lies next to one of them. Among the soldiers' bodies are embroidered the bright red drops of their spattered blood.

I backtrack among the images of the chimerical city and the experimental playfulness of the forms of the human body, and head outside to the Séptima, where loud salsa music from a nearby shoe store jolts me back into the busy late Saturday afternoon.

The heavy wooden door to the exhibition is once again closed, an invisible door behind which I have caught a glimpse of visible dreams and the oft-invisible war.

Dogs II

A group of homeless dogs squat together on a blanket in front of a handicrafts shop on the Séptima. There's a tin can alongside the dogs, and a sign that tells passersby, "We live on the streets; that's why we're called street dogs." A worker comes by with paint-stained pants and squats down beside the dogs with some leftover bread. A few coins shine in the can. A human being is obviously attached to these dogs.

I wonder for a minute if this is a fairly sophisticated form of begging, with the coins ending up in human pockets. It's the first public reference I've seen to street dogs since I've been back in Bogotá, and I started asking friends about them.

"There are plenty of street dogs in Kennedy," says my friend Adriana, a doctor I've known since she was a little girl. She works in a clinic in the south of the city and drives through Kennedy, a working-class neighborhood named after the assassinated U.S. president. The neighborhood has Bogotá's highest homicide rate. I haven't gone to Kennedy in many years. I used to go a lot. Sacred Heart priests ran the diocese there, many of them from Spain and the United States. They also had a diocese in the highlands of Guatemala, and I witnessed their pain as their fellow priests in Central America were murdered one by one. I should go back to Kennedy to see the priests, if they are still there, but I'm not ready for revisiting the remnants of pain. I take Adriana's word on the dogs.

"They kill them," Consuelo tells me. She's the sister of a friend and is fast becoming a friend herself. "They round them up and kill them. They do it to human beings; why shouldn't they do it to dogs?" Her voice is bitter, and her reference is to alleged "*limpieza social*," or "social cleansing," the extermination of drug addicts or street children by right-wing groups or paramilitary forces.

Another friend tells me that a doggie census took place just before I arrived in Colombia in August. I find the report on the Internet. The figures are startling: 775,000 dogs in Bogotá, according to the Bogotá Health Department. That's one dog for every ten residents of the city. And 90,000 of these canines are street dogs.

So there are street dogs. I just don't see them, even though my friends and work cut through a wide swath of this city. And there is indeed a program to round up the animals, sometimes as many as several hundred a day. The dogs are held for five days to see if anyone claims them. The "pretty" or thoroughbred dogs and animals under a year old are offered in adoption, according to the Health Department. The rest are given lethal injections. Back in 1996 the street dogs used to be electrocuted, until the Animal Defense League raised a ruckus. Some 1,500 dogs are now put to sleep monthly. That's why I don't see the dogs on the streets.

The Bogotá Health Department conducts public health campaigns to offer free rabies shots and dog sterilization, with 270 stations in public parks. There's even an independent association of volunteer veterinarians called the Red Pawprint—La Huella Roja—that go to the populous poor neighborhoods in the south of the city to sterilize dogs.

I study the dog census. It includes the highly trained security dogs that we manage not to notice anymore, part of the normalized routine of antiterrorism, and the dogs that search for drugs at the airport and bus terminal. It includes the German shepherds and Labradors of an anti-alcohol brigade that sniff out clandestine liquor and weapons at concerts and football games. It encompasses the domestic pets and the stray dogs, the mascots of the very rich and the very poor. Even with public health measures, the canine population in Bogotá is growing 5 percent a year.

I think about the dog walkers I have seen. Some of the growth in thoroughbred dogs, *de raza*, is undoubtedly a trickle-down effect of the invisible drug money flowing into the city. I decide to do some strolling with my fingers, as the ad for the Yellow Pages says in the States, and find a doggy bus that transports the animals to a rural playground just outside the city. And there's a canine matrimonial agency that explains it's not just for breeding dogs; it's so the dogs don't feel lonely. According to an article in *El Tiempo*, three thousand dogs have been wed in the past five years.

I also find a funeral home for dogs, a dog resort, and a dog health spa, plus dozens of listings for dog trainers and dog walkers. Dogs get plastic surgery here. Their owners fix their ears and beautify their tails. Some dogs have corrective braces for their teeth.

The local supermarket, a middle-class bastion in a somewhat eclectic neighborhood, stocks imported pet food and rubber bones. Dog owners, along with the professional dog walkers, enjoy the park next to my house, the Parque de la Independencia, before and after work.

Dogs cut across classes here. It may be the very wealthy who send their dogs to a spa, and the very poor who use their dogs for body heat, but it is often the middle class who own dogs for company and security.

When I arrived in Bogotá many years ago, most everyone—even some relatively poor people—had a live-in maid. I didn't like the idea, and most of my friends and acquaintances thought I was pretty strange not to want this service. For me, it represented a loss of privacy and a shadow of slavery. Now hardly anyone has live-in maids. It's a combination of factors, my friends explain: people distrust strangers in their homes because of kidnappings and other acts of violence; maids could belong to one illegal faction or another; and fewer women are willing to live in someone else's home. New apartments are constructed without maid's rooms. Dogs provide the security that maids used to, of having "someone" in the house.

And dogs provide company. In the 1970s and 1980s, most of my friends lived with their parents until they got married, and sometimes even afterwards. Friends who came from the coast and other parts of Colombia most often lived in student residences or group apartments. Some still do, but living alone is now considered quite normal. But living by oneself can be lonely, and dogs have become popular as company and also as a way to meet other people. I don't know if that's globalization or modernization or if it's because Bogota has become a sprawling megacity, but dog ownership is now a part of the middle-class way of life.

I look back at the doggy census to see if it breaks down dog ownership by income group. It doesn't. But I notice that it lists the places where street dogs are abundant: Usme, Bosa, Kennedy, Suba, and Ciudad Bolívar—all far-flung working-class and poor neighborhoods at the very end of bus routes.

My eyes linger over the words "Ciudad Bolívar." I had been there the other day with a priest friend, Leonel, to look at a project. I had seen teenaged kids stumbling drunk along the unpaved streets that afternoon. I had seen children enjoying an exercise class and had talked to a displaced woman from Tolima—a refugee from the violence—about her spectacular vegetable garden. And yes, I had seen the dogs and also the roosters and a horse and even a pig. And when I think back on the experience, the dogs were as mangy and as thin as I used to see them on the downtown streets of Bogotá. Only they were somewhere else. And I hadn't noticed.

A City of Many Hues

The maid broke my handcrafted sauce spoon carved out of a coconut shell, a gift from friends in the western part of Colombia. I was furious and yet didn't want to be furious, because she is an excellent helper. White, I might add, the daughter of farmers from the mountainous region from Boyacá and unaware that sturdy coconut from the coast, when hammered into a spoon, can be quite fragile.

I saw the accident as irreplaceable damage. I have no plans to go to the Pacific Coast before I leave Colombia in two months. So I made a pro forma journey to a nearby handicrafts bazaar. Surprisingly, I found a decent replacement within five minutes.

I shouldn't have been surprised. In the twenty-two years since I left Bogotá, the city has transformed into a racially mixed metropolis. The country has evolved from one of strong regions, each with a centrifugal pull on the surrounding areas, to the traditional Latin American pattern of a predominant capital city.

Every time I walk down the Séptima, I am reminded of Bogotá's many hues. And I'm often impressed by how many dark-skinned people also look prosperous—lawyers with briefcases, businessmen with suits and ties, the gregarious owners of the local fish restaurants. And then there are those who look obviously poor and out of place, the recent arrivals from the war zones.

The shift to a racially mixed city permeates Bogotá life in myriad little ways, including finding a coconut-carved sauce spoon. The diversity is reflected in dance performances, music, restaurants, and handicrafts. It's also the realization that the further north one goes towards the prosperous stretches of malls and upscale restaurants, the less the mix.

Of course, as a North American in Bogotá, I'm seeing through the lens of my own particular view of racial diversity. When I arrived here in 1975, my closest friends were from the coastal cities of Barranquilla and Santa Marta. They were an olive color, a light tan, a darkish white, but I thought of them as my *costeño* friends, not any particular color at all. One of them moved to Washington, D.C., to take a job as a director in Latino theatre. When I visited him, he commented to me about a close friend from Barranquilla, "You know, here, she would be just another black." I wondered if he was also talking about himself.

In the United States, a black is someone with just a drop of African heritage, from charcoal black to light tan to fair with curly Afro-American hair. In Colombia, the term applies to only the darkest part of the spectrum or, perhaps increasingly, someone who identifies herself as a black person for political reasons. It's not unusual to find a charcoal-dark person and a blue-eyed blond one in the same family, and the lighter one would never think of himself as "passing" in identifying himself or herself as white.

Language is much more blatant in Colombia: a white person is a *mono*, which means "blondie," rather than its usual Latin American sense of "monkey"; a plump woman is a *gordita*, and a black person is a *negro* or *negrito*, and all those terms are used to address the other person directly in terms of endearment. The first time someone called me *gordita* many years ago, I went on a crying jag. I took it to mean "fatty," with all the U.S. stigma. Now I don't even notice when someone uses these terms. But I wonder whether it means that Colombians are race-blind or race-conscious by using this vocabulary as just one more physical description of the person they are talking to.

It's confusing to me, because Colombia is not race-blind. It's just a different type of myopia. Blacks in general are from the Atlantic and Pacific coasts, much of which are underdeveloped.

In the recent census, Afro-Colombian organizations called upon black-descent Colombians to identify themselves as such. They launched a campaign with noted Afro-Colombian artists, models, beauty queens, and sports figures, to encourage a positive checking off the "black" category of the census. The campaign was taken seriously; the National Statistics Department, known by its Spanish acronym "DANE," publicized the campaign. In the 1993 census, only 493,170 citizens identified themselves as black. The 2006 census figures on ethnic categories have not been released yet but, despite the campaign, are bound to be far less than the 26 percent of Colombians estimated by Afro-Colombian organizations. It's important, they say, to have the numbers so cultural and socioeconomic conditions can be taken into consideration.

I remember that the word "Afro-Colombian" wasn't used

when I lived here before. The Constitution of 1991 recognizes Colombia as a multicultural and multiethnic state, and that made a big difference in self-perception. In turn, the constitution gave rise a law known as Ley 40, which recognizes Afro-Colombians as a distinct ethnic group and establishes their territorial, cultural, economic, political, and social rights.

My head as reeling as I research the emergence of Afro-Colombian identity. The sun is shining outside, a warm presence after days and days of rain. I decide to take a walk through the park to clear my head. Instead, I'm managing to take an informal census without intending to: dark black, probably from the Chocó region in the Pacific; light tan, a mix of black, indigenous, and white features; darker tan; almost white; yellowish tan with indigenous features; white with a slight hue of indigenous; another dark black, but the facial features suggest the Atlantic Coast and a mix of something else, maybe Lebanese or even Chinese.

In the United States, almost certainly, the park-strollers would be considered black. Here—generally, but not always—the darker, the lower the socioeconomic class. A very high percentage of war refugees are Afro-Colombians, particularly from the Pacific region.

I think back on a day in Ciudad Bolívar a few months ago. Ciudad Bolívar is a crowded shantytown on the edge of Bogotá, with many dirt streets and with water pumped into the hilliest parts of the slum through clandestine makeshift tubes. It is a neighborhood of war refugees from all over the country, urban denizens with strong rural roots. I attended a kids' yoga class in the diocesan hall. And my eye was caught by two toddlers, a pale white girl in tattered red overalls and neat blond braids and a charcoal black boy with nappy hair, in blue jeans, a yellow sweatshirt, and red sneakers. They were holding hands. They were intently watching the yoga class with the gentle casualness of childhood friendship.

Now it crosses my mind as I write about the changing hues of Bogotá: in the poverty of displaced people living their childhood together in the same neighborhood, in the hope of families of all colors struggling to better their lives, in the struggle to emerge from difficult economic conditions, perhaps I have seen the future.

Robberies

The bus chase looked like a scene from a third-rate crime movie.

Three armed men had just robbed a woman who had withdrawn a considerable amount of money from the bank. She was carrying the money in manila envelopes and a small black suitcase, thinking that no one had seen her make the withdrawal. The men put a gun to her head, snatched the money, and threw her to the ground.

A policeman saw the incident. He called for reinforcements. The robbers boarded a bus headed for downtown Bogotá and ordered the driver to change his route. Thus began the chase, the images captured for evening television. When the police tried to surround the bus, the robbers shot the driver dead, and one of the robbers took the wheel. Another began to throw money out of the window. Finally a motorcycle cop intercepted the bus and killed one of the robbers. The other policemen entered and captured the remaining thieves. No passengers were hurt.

Watching fragments of the chase on television, I thought of Bogotá's reputation as a crime capital. When I lived here the first time, little street urchins called *gamines* would snatch necklaces and earrings, sometimes damaging earlobes and allegedly chopping off fingers to obtain wedding rings from reluctant victims. I've known women with torn earlobes but have never been able to figure out if the wedding-rings story is an urban legend or a gruesome fact.

In all my years as resident or visitor to this city, I've been robbed only once. That was almost thirty years ago, and the robbery had a nice ending. I was walking early Sunday morning up behind the Hilton Hotel to the offices of the Jesuit think tank CINEP for an anniversary commemoration of the death of guerrilla priest Camilo Torres. I went to CINEP quite often, as the priests were an excellent source of information on human rights abuses and social inequality. What I didn't think about that bright morning was that I never went to the offices on Sundays.

The young men came out of nowhere. I didn't see their faces, but they practically tumbled me as they snatched my purse and dashed off into the poor neighborhood above the Hilton known as La Perseverancia. I was shaken. I wanted to cry. I didn't have much money in my purse, and I didn't yet have any credit cards, but my keys and identification and even my invaluable address book were in my pocketbook. Besides, I loved my leather purse.

I walked into CINEP with a look on my face that alerted the priests to some sort of trouble. One of them asked what had happened, and when I told him, he said, "You are our guest. That can't happen." Yes, I thought, but it did. The next thing I knew, two priests were accompanying me into the neighborhood. They kept talking to people and telling them that I was their friend and that I had come to a special Mass for Camilo Torres. The next thing I knew, a wizened woman appeared. She was dangling my purse in her hands and handed it to one of the priests. Nothing was missing from my pocketbook. We walked back to CINEP, and the anniversary celebration had just begun.

I guess I've just been lucky. However, the bus escapade made me wonder about other people's experiences with robberies. My totally unscientific survey proved that *bogotanos* do get robbed and that robberies are divided into violent and nonviolent categories, clever and mundane.

People are always talking about how taxi drivers take their customers off to remote areas and rob them or how passengers are made to go from ATM to ATM to withdraw money. The U.S. Embassy sent out a warning to resident citizens to use only radio taxis rather than hailing cabs on the street. I don't know a single person who has been robbed that way, in what's called a *paseo millonario*. I'm not saying this type of robbery doesn't happen—just that my informal poll produced no examples.

On the other hand, I can tell you that taxi drivers are frequent victims of robberies, and clever ones at that. One cabdriver, a middle-aged man who described himself as "very careful" in selecting passengers, picked up a well-dressed young man in front of the Clínica San Rafael, in the southern part of Bogotá. At first he thought the man was a nurse since he was well-groomed and articulate. Then he noticed the limp. The young man explained that he had just come from a treatment for his ankle and that he had difficulty walking. He asked the driver if he knew where a certain barrio was, and the driver said no. The passenger offered to guide him, apologizing because the neighborhood was so close by.

The ride was only about five minutes long, and the young man had the driver stop near an alley. "Usually, I walk in; my house is right there," said the passenger. "But it's really hard for me to walk. Would you mind driving in?" So the driver did, and three thugs entered the car from each side and robbed him of his day's earnings, his car radio, and his leather jacket.

The hospital modus operandi is apparently quite common. Another driver told me of picking up a young, attractive woman in front of a hospital clinic in a fashionable part of Bogotá. She told him that her infant daughter was sick and that she had been dealing with insurance issues before she could bring her to a clinic in the southern part of the city. Would the driver mind stopping at her house to pick up the child and then going on to the clinic? The driver pulled up to a house in a neighborhood called Las Cruces and waited outside for the woman to fetch her child. Instead, two armed men came out and robbed him of all his money. He drove off to the nearest police station. The robbers obviously didn't expect him to return, because they were still in the house and still had almost all of his money when he returned with the law. Missing was about 100,000 pesos—some US$50—which apparently had been the "mother's fee" for luring him into the trap.

Collusions between bank employees and robbers aren't unheard-of either. One engineer was in the bank, cashing a hefty check for his services. The teller apologized profusely, saying that there wasn't enough money available since the armored truck had just picked up a delivery. She told him to go to another bank, where there would be easy parking and enough money. In the bank parking lot, a man came from the right and another from the left, both armed with knives. The engineer handed over the money and drove off.

And then there are the pickpockets. A friend of mine has been robbed not once, but twice, of her wallet and cell phone as she rode in the elevator on the way up to the movie theatre at the top of the elegant Atlantis mall. By now she's figured out there's a ring of women thieves operating there. Pickpockets also love the TransMilenio because it's almost always crowded. One of the first sign-language gestures that I learned when I came to Bogotá was scratching the cheek. That meant "Look out; someone's trying to rob you."

The cries of "¡Páralo, páralo!"—"Stop him, stop him!"—are hardly ever heard on the Bogotá streets now since the *gamines* have disappeared. The cries are a way to call attention to the thief without directly getting involved. I was about to write that casual street robberies had been replaced by pickpocketing and planned armed robberies. But then my friend and neighbor Liliana came home to say that a middle-aged thief had snatched her gold chain and medallion on the Séptima. She had forgotten to take it off, a common precaution. She went running after the thief, and the cries of "¡Páralo, páralo!" began to accompany her. A policeman intercepted the thief; the chain was hidden under the robber's tongue. But the medallion had fallen someplace on the sidewalk, and cop, victim, and thief returned to the scene of the crime to scour the street and search for the medallion. It had disappeared.

So much for informal surveys about vanishing street crime. A news item appeared in *El Tiempo* a few days afterwards, citing the magazine *Revista Criminalidad*, and based on statistics from the criminal investigation directorate (DIJIN). Homicides are on the decline in Colombia, but the number of robberies has increased significantly in the past year: 41,215 robberies in 2005, up from 28,611 the previous year. Kidnapping is also way down, and car and motorcycle theft is also declining. Home invasions are about the same: 14,777 cases, 36 fewer than in the previous year.

The statistics also showed that in 2004 there were 46 massacres in Colombia in 2004, with 263 victims, and in 2005 there were 48 massacres, with 252 victims. The latter figures were encountered in the thirteenth paragraph of a fifteen-paragraph story, a buried reminder that a Colombian police blotter is sometimes no ordinary one.

Random Acts of Kindness

The coffee was always strong and steaming, so I liked to stop at the little bakery in the late afternoon after class. Journalism workshops exhaust me, and the students at the Mariana University in Pasto were bright, inquisitive, and demanding. Coffee, more than a drink, was a pause before returning to the hotel to prepare for the next day.

I lingered by the cash register, waiting for my change. The cashier was hardly more than a teenager, and I commented how much I liked her handcrafted beaded earrings. "Thank you. Where are you from?" was the inevitable question, with me replying with an almost true response: "I live in Bogotá. I'm originally from the United States." And then adding that I was teaching at the Mariana that week. I took my change and began to cross the wide avenue back to my hotel.

I waited on the strip in the middle of the avenue for an opportunity to cross. The traffic whizzing by was about as heavy as in Bogotá, but traffic lights and crosswalks were scarce. I think about how traffic has become less chaotic in Bogotá because of city planning and mass transportation, and I muse a bit on how I could incorporate that experience into a journalism lesson. I feel a presence beside me. A quiet, slow presence. I am about to be robbed, I think, and there is nowhere to dash off to.

Startled, I look up. The teenage cashier from the bakery was beside me, slightly out of breath. My first thought was that she had given me too much change and was now reclaiming the difference. I should have counted the change. I looked down. In her extended hand were the black-and-white beaded earrings that I had admired. "These are for you," she explained. "A memory of Colombia." She paused, remembering that I lived in Bogotá. "A memory of Pasto," she smiled.

They weren't expensive earrings, and I decided to accept the gift, moved by the random act of kindness. Pasto, near Ecuador's border, has a small-town feel. The shops still close at midday for two hours for lunch, and almost all of my students went home to eat and rest. At first, I saw the young woman's kindness as a reflection of the provincial atmosphere. But then I realized that my life in Bogotá has also been marked by random acts of kindness.

Living in a student residence with some Honduran friends when I first arrived in 1975, I liked to go to a nearby restaurant that served arepas—thin white corn pancakes—with broiled meat. Customers sat around a horseshoe-shaped counter that made it easy to meet other students and neighbors. One day the waitress was particularly attentive, filling my coffee cup and bringing me an extra portion of the homemade spicy sauce *ají casero*. I left a small tip beside my plate and walked off.

The waitress came dashing out, "Señorita, señorita, you forgot your money." Tips weren't common, and I later learned that if you were moved to leave a tip, you handed it to the waiter or waitress. I explained that I meant the money as a tip, and she smiled, but refused the gratuity.

Gifts of earrings or refused tips might seem trivial, slight acts of cordiality toward a pleasant foreigner. As I return to Bogotá after more than twenty years, I perceive that this civility permeates society. It coexists with and contradicts the country's reputation for violence. The sense of kindness and service is embedded in the language. "Con mucho gusto," "a la orden," and "de nada" are all phrases that indicate that pleasure is involved in being attentive. Some people say the phrases routinely, maybe even most people, but there's often a soft smile and a lingering on the vowels that tell me that the person is really enjoying being of service.

Little gestures pop up so frequently that, after a while, I don't notice them. When I first arrived back in Bogotá, I needed to get some instant photos taken for my *cédula*, my Colombian identity card. A woman in her twenties was eating an ice cream cone that almost looked vanilla, but not quite. Curious about the off-white color, I asked her if the ice cream was vanilla. She replied that it was *ronpope*, rum raisin, and immediately gave me a little taste.

Recently, I was walking down the street with a friend when I heard some hissing in back of us. We kept walking and conversing until the hissing just became too persistent. My friend looked back, and two young gentlemen in business suits extended a 20,000-peso bill (about US$9) to my friend. "You dropped this," they explained and walked off into the crowded Bogotá streets before she could barely blurt out a thank-you.

In the buses, seated passengers often offer to hold books or shopping bags or even the babies of those standing. On the streets, there is a constant awareness of others: "Excuse me, but your child's sweater is dragging." "Your pocketbook is unzipped. Someone might rob you." "You forgot your umbrella."

In stores, people routinely "donate" a hundred pesos (about five U.S. cents) so that a fellow customer won't have to break a big bill or give back a purchase.

The civility seems deeply ingrained, and I think that's hopeful for building community and democracy, because of the sense of collectivity, of mutual kindness. And yet mutual suspicion lingers on the surface, until a situation is proved safe. Ask people for directions on the street, and their bodies will freeze slightly until they hear the university-bred voice or the foreign accent, an assurance that this is not a robbery. I experience this situation over and over again, on the streets and on the bridges of Bogotá.

I have vertigo. A dark dizziness and fear overcomes me in high places, and I feel the traffic swirl below and the ground move beneath me. Vertigo wasn't much of an issue for me in the 1970s and 1980s in Bogotá, but now the city is filled with long pedestrian bridges that keep traffic moving. I often try to convince myself that my vertigo is psychological, and get up my courage to cross the bridges. Sometimes I make it across the bridge. Sometimes I get stuck in the middle, unable to move forward, unable to move back, watching the traffic and getting dizzier and dizzier.

I watch people watch me. I watch them wonder if this is a ploy, if somehow their wallet or watch will get tossed to an accomplice below. And someone inevitably breaks the anonymity of scurrying safety. "Can I help?" The helper is often a student or a middle-aged woman, sometimes a couple. I explain my vertigo, and I see my gringa accent comforts them. But they didn't know I was a foreigner before they asked. Sometimes they are headed in the other direction, as the bridges extend to opposite sides of the highway. That doesn't matter. There's always space for one more random act of kindness.

Upstairs, Downstairs

Every time I get my gas bill, I think about how people define themselves by socioeconomic class in Colombia.

That's because my public utilities—electricity, telephone, and water, as well as gas—are highly subsidized. In other words, I'm *estrato* 1 (stratum 1). Ordinarily, the subsidies for *estrato* 1 are reserved for the poorest of the poor, those who live in the sprawling hillside slums encircling the city. However, I live in a downtown building that's historic patrimony, one of Bogotá's first apartment buildings. We're also categorized as stratum 1 as an incentive to keep middle-class people in the downtown area.

As in the case of my building, socioeconomic stratum is determined by one's neighborhood or the buildings within the neighborhood, rather than one's individual income. Still, historic preservation aside, strata are a pretty good indication of social class. Strata range from 1 to 6. Stratum 6 lives in the elegant and expensive new high-rises in the city's northern stretches, next to the malls that sell Armani and OshKosh. Strata 3 and 4 are the comfortable middle class in residential neighborhoods. The system is an equitable way of subsidizing public services, but it's also a constant reminder of blatant inequalities. I recall a headline in *El Tiempo* (March 31, 2006) about Colombia's aqueduct system: "Bogotá is like Switzerland and Chocó is like Angola." The same might be said of class differences within this city of seven million, and I'm reminded of that in each and every utility bill.

The official stratum system didn't exist when I lived in Bogotá in the 1970s and 1980s, even though the city was even more stratified than now. When I first came, I remember going to government offices and waiting and waiting, while secretaries paid attention to others. I didn't want to be rude, so I didn't open my mouth. I just waited patiently. I found the situation confusing, because the secretaries often seemed to make a point of not paying attention. Yet, when they finally did get to me, they seemed slightly embarrassed—as if they were the victims of a mistake or an oversight. One day I asked a friend to make some sense of the situation. "What are you wearing when you go to the offices?" she asked. "I wear a dress and some flats and, of course, my *ruana*, to keep warm."

A *ruana* is a blanket-type poncho woven out of virgin sheep wool. Mine was white and thick, nubs of virgin wool creating a complicated texture. I was in love with my *ruana*; I found it so elegant and comfortable.

"That's the problem," my friend diagnosed. "You don't open your mouth, and the secretaries think you're some peasant from

Boyacá." That's when I learned the phrase *los de ruana*, the lower-class people, the stratum 1 before the system existed, the ones the secretaries don't pay any attention to.

I'm short for someone from the United States, just five feet tall, and my fondness for walking keeps my complexion ruddy in this mountain air. And people from Boyacá often have fair complexions and light eyes; I understood how I could have been confused with a peasant from the mountainous region north of Bogotá.

I was reminded of this class confusion the other day in yoga class in a dance studio right near my apartment. Most yoga classes are up north—where the stratum 6 people live—and I knew if I signed up for a distant class, I'd always find an excuse not to go. My nearby yoga class is on the top floor of a parking garage with a view of the mountains, and the teacher, Sebastián, is energetic and an excellent instructor. The only problem is that almost everyone else in the class is a dancer, and almost everyone else is at least thirty years younger than I am.

Still, I keep going. Sebastián is good at giving me an alternative exercise when the dancers contort themselves into pretzel shapes. I spot another woman in the class who is apparently not a dancer. She's a bit more experienced than I am, but her body does not bend and flow like the dancers. She is shorter than me, with a full-figured body and slightly crooked teeth. I ask Yolanda how long she has been taking the class, and she tells me that she has been at it three years, and encourages me to stick with it.

When the class finishes, I change into my street clothes and chat with the studio manager for a while in the office. I walk back into the studio to take the stairs through the parking garage. Yolanda is sweeping the floor. She is the cleaning woman.

One might say that dancers and yoga practitioners are a special group, willing to welcome a cleaning woman into yoga class just as readily as they welcome a clumsy middle-aged gringa. Yet, despite my gas bill, I think huge societal changes are taking place here, and I struggle to understand them. The social breach is as great as ever. According to recent figures from the Secretaría de Hacienda Distrital (District Treasury Department), 40 percent of the city's wealth is in the hands of 7 percent of its population. Sixteen percent of Bogotá's residents belong to stratum 4, 5, or 6, while 84 percent struggle to cover their basic needs, according to the report.

Yet there is something different now about the concept of class in Colombia. Even the language is less rigid. In my *primera ronda*, almost everyone except close friends were *usted*, the formal way of saying "you." I was always conscious of that because I had learned my Spanish in a Dominican neighborhood in New York where just about everyone was *tú*, the informal way of saying "you." My friends from Colombia's Atlantic Coast back then called me and everyone else *tú*, but the folks from Bogotá were decidedly more formal. Now *tú* is rampant, except in very formal occasions.

Dress has changed. When I lived in Bogotá before, I often saw *cachacos*, traditionally dressed gentlemen in suit, vest, tie, hat, and brightly shined shoes, with a handkerchief tucked neatly into a suit pocket and carrying a cane or umbrella. *Cachacos* can still be spotted among the sea of jeans and pantsuits, but dress has also been democratized. *Los de ruana* are more likely to be wearing faded jeans and a worn leather jacket than the thick poncho.

I'm coming back with a friend from lunch in the colonial Candelaria section of town, when she spots a neatly dressed young woman near her office. She greets the woman, probably a young college student who is helping out part-time, and discusses some concerns about a schedule. As the young woman walks away, my friend explains, "That's my maid's daughter."

My own maid's daughter is an accountant. The son of a friend's maid has managed to purchase a taxicab. And in addition to this anecdotal evidence of social mobility, even the phenomenon of maids is transforming in Bogotá.

The construction of new apartments didn't contemplate maid's rooms, as space becomes more expensive per square meter. Ironically, better enforcement of labor laws to benefit live-in maids also helped do away with this source of employment. The latest 2005 census found that only 0.5 percent of Colombian households now have live-in maids. The number may be slightly underreported to avoid paying for Social Security and insurance, but my daily life seems to confirm the dramatic decrease. I know absolutely no one with a live-in maid, although some of my friends do have a maid that comes on a daily basis, and even more that have a maid that comes once or twice a week.

So while I'm being reminded about social class with my gas bill, fewer Colombians—and far fewer *bogotanos*—are still ringing little silver bells to let the maid know it's time to serve breakfast.

What seems to have changed is not so much social class as social mobility. Inequalities are still rampant. The cycle of poverty is insidious and persistent, constantly fueled by war refugees. Children still go to *escuelas*, overcrowded public schools, or *colegios*, elite private schools, and you can still most often tell who's who by their last name or the stratum on their gas bill.

Yet there is at least an illusion of social mobility that didn't exist before. In addition to the democratization of dress that I was musing on earlier, there's also some democratization in material goods. In the 1970s and 1980s, electronic goods such as televisions, washing machines, computers, and microwave ovens were extremely expensive. The rich bought them without thinking. The middle class bought them on the black market or in shopping excursions to the duty-free island of San Andrés. The poor were excluded.

The cost of electronic goods has dropped drastically as Colombia has moved into an open trade market. In addition, credit is easy to get. Large discount stores like Alkosto are popular among all classes. And even when a poor family cannot afford a computer, Internet services at cybercafes and public libraries make computer use accessible. An enterprising company has even started a mobile washing machine service in Bogotá's marginal neighborhoods. If you can't afford a washing machine, you can rent one in your own home at a reasonable cost.

Democratization of dress and consumerism isn't really closing the social breach, but it does make class differences less obvious. And that encourages class mobility, as does the ability to emigrate and send earnings back home, not to mention the mobility of the drug-trafficking culture. People can reinvent themselves, and sometimes they even are forced to reinvent themselves. That's certainly the case of the *desplazados*. The class mobility can be downward for war victims, but as attested by the many fish restaurants in Bogotá founded by owners from the Pacific Coast, the city sometimes and eventually provides a way to reinvent oneself and allows upward mobility.

Perhaps downward mobility itself contributes to the strengthening of mobility within the class system. I talk with an energetic short-haired woman in her fifties who sells cheese in the local market. In Boyacá, the rural, mountainous region north of Bogotá, her family owned cows and chickens and fine horses with saddles, as well as ample crops of corn and potatoes and fruit trees. Her mother's cancer dug into the family coffer. Then guerrillas finished off any hopes of prosperity. The family fled to Bogotá.

Her four sons are all studying in high school and college, and her daughter works as a teacher's assistant. She doesn't know if she will ever return to the land. As I converse with the cheese vendor, I observe that her values are middle-class rural values. The stories are repeated again and again throughout Bogotá, the people who once had something. The dream is that education and hard work will bring back prosperity.

The hundreds of students who attend night school, both at the high school and university levels, attest to that relatively new belief in class mobility. Every evening at about 10 p.m., students with heavy book bags and knapsacks board buses and the Trans-Milenio for the journey home. Many of them have worked all day and then gone to evening classes, intent on getting ahead.

I came to Colombia for the first time at the height of the marijuana boom. One couldn't talk about class then without referring to the new rich and the old rich. The new rich were those who made their money off of drugs, dressed in infinitely bad taste, couldn't speak grammatically, and bought expensive homes or apartments, only to furnish them in a gaudy, outlandish fashion. The old rich were the ones with the right last names and a fine way of speaking and infinitely good and cultivated taste, at least according to the fellow members of their social class.

It's not that the distinction doesn't exist anymore. People have just stopped talking about it. New wealth has married old wealth or has simply acquired some education or at least made it possible for their kids to do so. There's still plenty of bad taste around, as drug barons look for ways to spend easily acquired money. I get into furious fights with Colombian friends about the effect of drug trafficking on class. Most of them say that—at least, in some cases—people no longer see hard work as the way to a good life. It's true that easy money, gang activity, and even recruitment by illegal armed groups tug at the old values, and it's hard to see which will win out. But I see the effect as more nuanced: drug trafficking, for better or worse, provides an example of social mobility. It breaks with Colombia's caste system.

So does emigration. Colombia traditionally is not a nation of emigrants. People flocked to the capital city or other urban centers, but, when I came to Colombia the first time, most of the emigration was to nearby Venezuela. And people working in Venezuela came home for the holidays and waited until they earned enough money in the oil-rich country to return home permanently. Now Colombians are flocking in large numbers to the United States and Spain, and they are sending money home to their communities. Remittances provide another source of wealth that is not dependent on class status.

In modern-day Bogotá, class is no longer fixed, I muse, thinking I should go pay my gas bill. It's class as determined by current socioeconomic status: class, not caste.

A young girl on a basic navy blue bicycle spins past me. She is concentrating, her mouth puckered, and she grinds to a shaky halt on the corner by the San Diego church. I ask her age, and she beams with pride. "Seven!" she tells me, and I congratulate her on her bike prowess. As I walk further along the *ciclovía*, Bogotá streets converted into an extensive Sunday bike path, I hear her tell her parents about my compliment. Actually, I'm somewhat envious.

I never learned how to ride a bicycle. In New York City and in Bogotá, when I lived here twenty-five years ago, bike riding was left to the valiant. As a child, I had managed to graduate from a tricycle to a bicycle with training wheels. However, my faulty sense of balance and incessant protests made my parents give up on the endeavor.

When I moved to Cambridge in 1997, I decided to try again, this time as a fifty-year-old woman. The Cambridge School for Adult Education offered a course in bike riding for adults. My classmates were all women: Muslim women, urban women who had never learned, and one lady in her seventies who never had a bicycle because of the Great Depression. The teachers were fabulous and patient, and I was learning well until one day, when I was getting off the bike, I lost my balance and fell hard on my coccyx. It took me a good six months before I could go up stairs without pain. I gave up my bicycle quest.

I often spend Sundays and holidays watching bike riders. That's because the *ciclovía* wends past my apartment. Although Bogotá has many bike paths on its streets, it shuts down major roads to traffic on Sundays and holidays. That's when, as the old revolutionary saying goes, "the streets belong to the people." According to *El Tiempo* (March 12, 2006), almost two million people use the seventy-five miles of bike paths each Sunday.

It's a carnival on wheels. And the *desfile*, the carnival parade, is not only bikers but skaters and walkers and runners too. There are bicycles and tricycles, racers and clunkers, scooters, baby carriages, and even an occasional wheelchair.

I wouldn't be able to tell the temperature by looking at *ciclovía* fashion. Bogotá may be eternal spring, but the bikers haven't figured out if that's raw March or sweltering May. Two guys in long hair dash by on their top-model bikes in black racer shorts and white T-shirts, and a bare-chested guy with very developed muscles swings past me on Rollerblades. Not to mention the stylish blond woman in her early twenties, promenading beside her bicycle, in a sports bra and culottes.

And then there are two women, not much older, racing along in blue jeans and thick wool sweaters. A girl who looks to be around ten years old pedals hard in her bright pink pants and a heavy turquoise sweatshirt, while a scantly dressed Barbie rides along in her handbasket. Two brothers on bicycles with training wheels wear heavy sweaters and woolen scarves draped across their faces as their parents give them pointers. It could be any type of weather.

The *ciclovía* is very much a family affair. A heavyset man with a handlebar mustache darts by with his son riding in a child's seat in the back. A girl around seven or eight tries to pedal while her older brother mounts in back of her, standing and fighting the rotating wheels. Purple and pink Barbie bikes are the rage, and I count at least a half dozen; the moms often look like Barbies themselves. Even the family dogs get into the act; a dog runs furiously on a leash alongside his owner-biker; another dog sits proudly in a red wagon pulled by a toddler.

Only a few of the bikers wear helmets. First aid stations and mobile bicycle repair shops, sponsored by the city, are scattered along the route. Volunteers in bright yellow jackets with the logo "Bogotá without indifference" monitor traffic on the cross streets where cars are permitted.

The *ciclovía* has been around for quite a while as a concept. It's different from the bike paths that some eighty-three thousand cyclists use every day as a means of transportation. Although they have their separate lanes on busy city streets, these riders must contend with belching smoke from buses, noise pollution, and careless motorcycles, cars, and even pedestrians. Sunday is different, an oasis of city space.

The first *ciclovía* was inaugurated on December 15, 1974, six months before I arrived in Bogotá. It was limited to part of the Séptima and the Carrera 15, but frankly I don't remember anyone who ever went. In 1982, Bogotá mayor Augusto Ramírez Ocampo, strengthened the *ciclovía*, extending it into many of the city's neighborhoods. It was only recently, under the Antanas Mockus administration, that the *ciclovía* became a citywide block party on Sundays. Mockus added miles and miles of bicycle routes, but he also inculcated a sense of civic responsibility and pride in the city's citizens.

I am reminded of that sense of civic responsibility as I gaze at the number of children whose parents are far ahead or behind them on their own bikes. In a city where everyone is wary that something unexpected is going to happen, everyone seems to know that nothing bad will happen at the *ciclovía*. It's community; it's the town plaza; it's joyous urban space.

It's a space for informal business too. A hefty man in a large straw hat grinds sugarcane in a vehicle that resembles an ice cream cart with two enormous wheels, like something directly modeled on a Rube Goldberg contraption. He sells the sugarcane juice, *guarapo*, to thirsty bikers. I watch him as he disposes of the waste pulp in a nearby garbage can, and think how the bike paths have succeeded in creating a sense of civic pride. That kind of garbage might have been tossed on the street before.

Not to be outdone in strange contraptions along the bike route, near the National Park, a man in an apron is selling *arepas de chocolo y queso*, fresh corn and cheese pancakes. He is cooking them with firewood in an oven on a cart on his bicycle.

The smell of the cooking arepas mixes with the eucalyptus of the park. On a Sunday the air is fresh, free from automobile and bus contamination.

Less exotic vendors are also hard at work. One guy sells sunglasses from a huge board. Even though the sun is barely shining, he has several customers. A woman calls out "Llamadas, llamadas, llamadas" in a rhythmic beat, selling minutes on a cell phone. Others sell fresh fruit with cream and coconut, a gummy white sweet called *gelatina*, candy, gum, and of course the ubiquitous ice cream. Yet it's not the commerce that dominates but the spirit of a public plaza, a public space to be enjoyed by all.

Folks race and dawdle and learn and mingle and meet. It's a festival on wheels. I'm not the only walker, and even though I never learned to ride a bike, I figure I'm just one more happy participant in Bogotá's *ciclovía*.

Bombs and Other Loud Noises

The loud noise shook the walls of the Fulbright office. Car alarms began to wail. Professors, students, and invited guests were serving themselves sandwiches and salad, chatting as we waited for the featured speaker. "It's a bomb," said one of the students. "It's thunder," I insisted.

Colombians and North Americans began to discuss the noise. The room was divided as to the cause of the noise, and it didn't divide evenly. Some of the Colombians thought it might be a bomb or maybe a gas explosion. Others thought it was a bomb. Lightning flared in the sky, and rain began to pour. "See, it was thunder," I said, ready to be granted my point. A student pointed to a cloud of smoke emanating from a neighborhood way off in the distance and said, "See, it was a bomb."

There was nothing on the radio, nothing in the newspaper the next day. The spiral of smoke could have come from burning wood. I think the noise was the prelude to the heavy electrical storm. But then again, I will never know for sure.

When I first moved into my apartment in Bogotá this fall, the main avenue in front of my house became a pedestrian mall for a night. Stores were open, clowns and musicians lined the sidewalks, and people thronged to gawk and shop. I wandered through the crowds for a bit and then went up to my apartment to answer some e-mail.

Suddenly I heard explosion after explosion, eruptions into the night sky. I strained to look out of my window, which faces the mountains rather than the main street. I couldn't see anything. I was afraid. The large gathering would be a perfect target for a terrorist attack. I couldn't see anything at all. I turned on the radio. Music was playing. I thought of calling my neighbors and remembered they had gone out for the evening. I looked out the window again.

There, over in the park adjacent to my apartment building, I saw workers and a group of children look up towards Colpatria, Bogotá's tallest building. I could barely see the expressions on their faces, but I recognized the happy awe. Fireworks. I went downstairs and watched the last of the red and yellow and green spirals explode into the night sky.

Bombs were far more frequent when I lived in Bogotá in the 1970s and 1980s, and they escalated in the 1990s after I left. In 2001 two bombs exploded outside a university here during morning rush hour, killing four people. In 2003 a bomb planted in the social club El Nogal took thirty-three lives and caused injury to almost two hundred more. A car bomb a few months later took the lives of six people in a busy shopping district. Later that year, grenades were thrown into the Bogotá Beer Company and another restaurant popular with U.S. military personnel, killing one woman and injuring seventy-one others.

Bombs in Bogotá are sometimes frequent, sometimes absent, but any loud unusual noise is a reminder of this tool of Colombia's armed actors: insurgent groups, paramilitaries, drug traffickers, and common delinquents.

A tire blows out in a city street, and the driver inevitably turns to the passenger and says, "Una llanta . . ."—a tire. Nothing more needs to be said. No explanations are needed.

I was on the way to a friend's wedding in a town in *tierra caliente*—the hot country. We stopped in the early evening to get soft drinks and to stretch. Several explosions were heard in the distance. It wasn't fireworks, and it wasn't lightning, and it certainly wasn't a tire blowing out. We looked at each other. The cashier saw us looking. "Tejo," she said.

Tejo, a modern version of the indigenous sport *turmequé*, is played in the countryside and poor barrios throughout Colombia. The game of *tejo* is quite possibly the only sport that involves explosives. Similar to American horseshoes, participants toss disks against a distant target that contains blasting caps. To win the game, a player must set off more blasting caps than his or her opponent.

So we weren't hearing bombs, but we were indeed hearing explosives.

Back in Bogotá, I take my usual Sunday jaunt through San Alejo, the flea market that operates in the parking lot next to my apartment building. I am leafing through old photographs of the city when I hear sirens. In the distance, I hear something exploding. "Algo hubo," says the vendor quietly. "Something's up." People keep shopping, but there is a quiet nervous murmur.

The next day, there's news in the paper about a gas explosion in an apartment building that killed six people, mostly university students. And the following day, the DAS—the Colombian version of the FBI—announces that they have found traces of explosives. They say that the students were killed while making bombs.

The radio was the way radios almost always are in Bogotá taxis, too soft for me to understand, too loud to tune out, and too crackly for comfort. I heard the word "TransMilenio" and the word "children" and the word "bomb." I couldn't believe what I was hearing. The TransMilenio, the five-year-old modern rapid transit system, is a source of pride for Bogotá and for Colombia. I asked the taxi driver to turn up the radio. I asked him what had happened.

A bomb had exploded on the TransMilenio a few minutes before, injuring several young boys going home from school. The news pierced through me, the shattering of an illusion. The TransMilenio is a symbol of modernization and of civic participation. *Bogotanos* used to push and shove to get onto buses. Now they wait in line. The TransMilenio has electronic signs announcing when the next bus is coming, and maps to show customers the routes. In a formerly chaotic city, the TransMilenio has established new orderly parameters.

I shivered. That the victims were children deepened the emotional impact. I can think of only two times the radio has dug such a deep hole into my heart: the assassination of John F. Kennedy and 9/11.

The citizens of Bogotá reacted, organizing protest vigils at TransMilenio stations in the early hours of the morning. Children marched in the pouring rain under gigantic umbrellas. Many of them dressed in black, the word *paz* (peace) painted on their cheeks. TransMilenio buses displayed electronic signs reading "No to Terrorism," and each bus carried a white flag.

Of the children injured, ten-year-old Daniel Beltrán died first, much of his little body covered with burns. His friends fondly called him "Dennis the Menace" because of his mischievous love of pranks. Bryan Romero, eleven, who had taken the bus as a way to pass time after school, died a day later.

In an April 8, 2006, editorial, *El Tiempo* reminded readers that as cruel as the bombing incident was, Daniel and Bryan were not alone in their fate as children: "The situation of children in Colombia is lamentable. The subject of childhood doesn't attract voters, and the politicians have other concerns. . . . (E)very effort should be made to make the theme of children and youth a part of the national and local agenda."

The editorial cited a governors' forum in Medellín on childhood, adolescence, and the environment. In Colombia, according to the forum's statistics, half of the 17 million children and youths under eighteen are poor; 16 of 100 suffer from malnutrition; 20,000 die yearly from causes that don't have to be fatal; and 10,000 suffer physical or mental abuse. In the past year, 5,691 children had been killed in Colombia, 60 percent of them under four years old.

In this society, where childhood is so precarious, it's often hard to tell the victims from the perpetrators. In the TransMilenio bombing, the alleged perpetrators were practically children themselves. Four young men in their early twenties, recruited by the FARC as urban militia, carried the homemade bombs in their backpacks, leaving the bomb-bottles on empty seats. The boys were curious, as children are, perhaps hoping to enjoy someone's forgotten soda pop. That's why, of twenty injured people, the most seriously injured were seven little boys.

For days, I got butterflies in my stomach when I boarded the TransMilenio. For weeks, I thought of Daniel's lively face and Bryan's cherubic look and the serious intensity of young girls parading in black with the word "peace" on their cheeks. And then the memories faded, as they do in Colombia, until the next time the radio blurts out another unexpected tragedy.

Dark rain clouds hovered over Monserrate's verdant peak. I scurried from the Olímpica grocery store towards my apartment to watch the theatre parade from my neighbor's window facing the Séptima. Much to my surprise, despite the threatening storm, the crowd was six deep. I couldn't get across the street. I was carrying bread and lemons—and my pocketbook. I don't like to be in crowds with my pocketbook.

The parade was to kick off Bogotá's International Theatre Festival, two weeks of drama, comedy, romance, classics, and improvisation from all over the world. This year's theatre festival featured Russia. I'd never been to the festival before. Held every two years, it started long after I left Colombia the first time around.

Toddlers, teenagers, elderly men and women, students, intellectual-looking couples from the North and shabby-looking couples from the South, folks in jeans, and office workers in suits surrounded me. Four hundred children from Colombia's Caribbean Coast, accompanied by actors on stilts, each waving the flags of the countries participating in the festival, led the way. The children in front of me applauded and screamed. The crowd let loose as a folklore troupe known as La Diablada de Oruro led thousands of actors and dancers and even cheerleaders. A woman dancer from Neiva swirled in her wide red skirt; a cheer went up as dancers from the Dominican Republic raised their machetes to the crowd. *Gigantonas*—huge papier-mâché figures—pranced on stilts. Young policemen in white-painted faces mingled with the crowd, and a giant dragon grabbed one of them and began to dance.

This wasn't a parade; it was a carnival. Parents began to pass their children over the heads of spectators to complete strangers so that the youngsters could watch from the front row. A tall man who had been partially blocking my view motioned to me to stand in front of him. White and red roses floated down from my apartment building in front, cheering on the participants. I let my purse dangle; my caution was gone. The clouds still threatened, but everyone now was together, enjoying the international floats and domestic folklore.

Neighborhood participation from Bogotá with musical bands from some of the city's more marginal neighborhoods, spectacular cheerleaders who outdid the finest gymnasts, children on stilts, and teenagers clowning brought screams of enthusiasm. Many friends and neighbors must have been in the audience, but the quality was high and the applause well deserved.

The parade went on and on. A few drops of rain began to fall. No one paid any attention. Dancers and actors were performing from all over Colombia: the carnival of "whites and blacks" from Pasto; machete-wielding cowboys from Quindío; a proud float of gypsies, blacks, whites, indigenous folk; *gaiteros* who play their traditional music from San Jacinto; huge butterfly dancers with pre-Columbian images; and even a staged clownish bullfight.

I couldn't help thinking how so many of the dancers came from regions where the conflict was still raging, wondering if some of them had lost brothers or fathers or sisters or daughters. I couldn't help thinking about how the white-faced police cadets looked so happy as they danced and clowned, and wondering if they could just as easily beat up a thief or a guerrilla suspect. They looked so fresh and young. Then I just stopped thinking, caught up in the collective joy.

A cry of jubilation spread through the crowd. A float was passing with festival founder Fanny Mickey, an Argentine Jewess with an outlandish crop of dyed red hair, an unlikely heroine. Arriving in Colombia more than forty years ago, she is now a national symbol. The applause wouldn't stop, and as the float passed into the distance, I couldn't help thinking of Nicaragua's Violeta de Chamorro, who managed to draw together her country after civil strife and bloody divisions. Maybe Mickey should be the next president—except, of course, she couldn't be and wouldn't want to be. (Mickey died in August 2008).

Then I understood. The people around me—even the police—
at least for now were citizens. They were active participants, and
the festival belonged to them, regardless of their race, age, creed,
class, or political affiliation. I was thinking too much again and
returned to gazing at the exotic martial arts of a Korean theatre
troupe. The parade lasted for almost two hours, and when it dis-
persed, I could finally cross the street. Reaching for the keys to
my apartment, I remembered to check my purse. Everything was
still intact.

For the next two weeks, I overindulged in theatre. I went to see
Chinese opera (for the first time in my life), a production called
Ciudad de Tebas, based on a Greek tragedy, in a theatre named
after Jorge Eliécer Gaitán, a Colombian leader murdered in 1948.
And just as the fight between the two brothers in the Greek tragedy and the subsequent suicide of Antigone set off a wave of violent suicides and lonely abandonment, Gaitán's murder sparked
the present seeds of violence in Colombia. I'm not sure the full
theatre made the political connections, but emotionally the con-
nection was there, how violence and revenge infiltrate the very
core of society.

I guess that's why I chose two versions of *Hamlet*—Spanish
and Colombian—and why the festival chose three productions
of *Hamlet* (the other was Brazilian) for this festival. Even though
I also saw an Ecuadoran monologue on a woman's life, a Chinese
opera based on a Greek tragedy, a Russian version of Chekhov's
Three Sisters, a Swiss version of *Don Juan*, and a carnivalesque Cuban performance about the French Revolution, I saw only a small
fraction of the theatre presented by 52 international companies
and 141 Colombian troupes. Theatre was everywhere, and a lot of
it was free. It was performed in the bullring, in the coliseum, and
in Bogotá's poorest neighborhoods, in twenty different parks and
in the streets and even on the TransMilenio. It was performed in
the elegant Teatro Colón with its chandeliers and gold trimming,
in the cavernous downtown Jorge Eliécer Gaitán theatre, and in
converted movie houses. Theatres were sold out, and parks were

crowded. There was street theatre and children's theatre and concerts and dance and a huge closing firework display.

From the very beginning of the festival with its huge parade, I felt a sense of *convivencia*, of belonging and participation throughout the city. People went to the performances in large groups, with their families, with their friends or alone—it didn't seem to matter, because of the sense of togetherness. Ah, yes, but I am a journalist by training and a cynic by temperament, and I couldn't help thinking whether the festival was bread and circuses for the tired public.

I felt as if columnist Óscar Collazos was reading my mind when he wrote in *El Tiempo* on April 6:

> The Theatre Festival is a huge fiesta that doesn't have anything to do with the "bread and circus" fed to the population. . . . It costs a lot to stage this event, it's true, but a lot less than it would cost if numerous theatre companies throughout the world did not accept to come and act in Colombia, a country "at war" in which, during 14 days, tens of thousands of citizens hurl themselves into the streets to respond to a collective act of participation in an immense celebration of the imagination, among the crossfire of spectacular fireworks.

I couldn't have said it better. Maybe the Colombian public has created its own particular version of the pacifist slogan of the 1960s. Only now it's "Make theatre, not war."

Red, Yellow, and Blue

My Colombian friend who loves to travel always used to carry a plastic Éxito bag. The popular supermarket bag with its distinctive black-and-yellow logo caught the attention of fellow Colombians in Europe, Asia, Africa, and the United States. And he would always manage to find a fellow Colombian.

The grocery bag was a symbol of Colombian identity. However, the symbol could be easily interpreted only by other Colombians. Strangers saw a supermarket bag, or just a traveller's plastic bag.

He wouldn't need that plastic bag today. Colombians are doting on their national symbols. Street vendors, handicraft shops, and even variety stores are selling red, yellow, and blue bracelets made from wool, thread, seeds, beads, straw, and even dyed orange peel. They sell red, yellow, and blue woven wool hats and scarves. Red, yellow, and blue are the colors of the Colombian flag.

Curious about these symbols, I go for a stroll down the Séptima. I spot a gentleman in a business suit wearing one of the bracelets, tucked discreetly under his watch. A college student carrying several heavy texts sports a red, blue, and yellow scarf. A woman in jeans pushing a baby carriage jangles several bracelets, at least three of them flag colors. It may be the most informal census in the world, but I'd say at least two out of every five persons are proclaiming their Colombian identity. The closer I get to the university, the numbers escalate.

And I'm only counting symbols with red, yellow, and blue. There are plenty of other Colombian symbols: T-shirts blazoned with images of the singers Shakira or Juanes or a famous Colombian soccer star with lots of hair whose name I forget. There's also one of Juan Valdez, the mythical coffee peasant with his burro. All these images are so well known that no names are printed on the T-shirts.

Fashion accessories such as tightly knitted bags with pre-Colombian designs that originated on the coast with the Arhuaco indigenous group, as well as earrings and necklaces that are replicas of objects in the Gold Museum, also promote Colombian identity. I didn't count those in my informal street survey either.

It's a Bogotá street, so the frequent symbols are not a case of Colombians identifying themselves to other Colombians in foreign lands. It's a way of saying, "Here we are."

When I lived in Europe in the 1990s, many Colombians responded that they were South American or Latin American when asked their origin. One even told me she was Andean. Of course, I recognize a Colombian accent when I hear one and could usually break through the reserve with a cautious, "From Bogotá or from Medellín?"

There were no obvious symbols. And most Colombians I knew were slightly ashamed of being Colombian. It meant being stopped at airports. It meant being somehow associated with drug lord Pablo Escobar. At best, it meant being considered a political exile when the real reason you were in Europe was to study literature or practice journalism or because you were married to a European.

At first I thought the answers were based on the caution that a U.S. person in Germany wouldn't have a clue about Colombia, just about Latin America. After all, Berlin had three "pan-Latino" restaurants run by Chilean exiles that served a panoply of cuisine ranging from Mexican enchiladas to Brazilian feijoada.

But even when I went to Bogotá on vacation to visit close friends, I found a kind of closet identity, always looking elsewhere, always downplaying what it is to be Colombian. At best I found some regional identity, a pride in being from the coast or from Medellín.

Now it's a different scene. Red, yellow, and blue are everywhere. In Bogotá the proliferation of Colombian symbols may have to do with the pride in the TransMilenio and positive urban development. It may be a way of saying, "I'm a citizen of the country, not just of my region," whether that be the coast or the jungle. It could be an outgrowth of the progressive 1991 Constitution, which spelled out citizens' rights in an unprecedented fashion.

The symbols remind me the ubiquitous peace symbols of my college days in New York, at once a protest and a sign of togetherness, of social healing. And they remind me of the American flags hanging in Cambridge in the days following the September 11, 2001, attacks on the Twin Towers. You had to read the flags as symbols by the way they were hung. Horizontal flags were patriotic: us versus them. Vertical flags were in solidarity with the pain and the losses, citizens consoling other citizens, a sign of mourning and peace.

I ask a friend if the Colombian symbols are patriotic, and he sniffs, "Patriotic is something else," referring to the president's Plan Patriótico that advocates "democratic security" measures.

I ask another friend about nationalism, and she snorts, "Nationalism is a dangerous thing. That's what led to Hitler." She always wears a red, yellow, and blue woven straw bracelet. "So why do you wear it?" I press. "Because I'm Colombian," she answers.

Disappeared

I'd seen him in the elevator of my building. I think. He worked with my neighbor, after all. Or was it a long time ago, with my friend Zita, the labor lawyer? Or maybe it was at the Javeriana University, where I sometimes go to conferences on history or literature.

The face on the poster stares out at me. The eyes are direct and catch mine, as the mouth crinkles into a half-serious smile. It is a strong face with rugged but gentle features set off by unruly hair and a bulky mustache that somehow seems pasted on.

I know I've seen him someplace before. What one generally does is ask. Sometimes people don't remember: was it thirty-one years ago when I first came to Colombia, or was it only the other day on the elevator going up to my apartment? And now I wonder if I will ever get the opportunity to ask.

Even before his disappearance, Jaime Enrique Gómez Velásquez wasn't that well known. He was a history professor, a union activist, and an adviser to the political candidate past and future, the senator and my neighbor Piedad Córdoba.

"Aparezca Jaime," the poster reads. I fret over how to translate that. "Appear, Jaime!" sounds like a circus act. "Make Jaime appear!" is not much better, and "Free Jaime" implies the certainty that he is indeed kidnapped or being held in a secret prison somewhere.

Gómez had gone out to jog early in the morning of March 21, 2006, as he always did. He never returned. He had become one of the disappeared.

The International Committee of the Red Cross in its annual report says that families have reported 317 new cases of forcible disappearances in 2005, adding to the 279 cases the previous year. That's a total of 596 new disappearances.

I look at the posters of Jaime as I stroll down the Séptima on the way to a lunch date. The posters remind me that the Red Cross figures don't include this year, 2006. They don't include silent disappearances, those that have not been reported by family members.

It is beginning to rain, a cold April drizzle. I look up at the green mountains that surround my adopted city; clouds are spreading over Monserrate until the green becomes an impressionist painting of fogged pastel. The posters are summoning people to a rally. Jaime's daughter is speaking to a small gathering, talking about her father, imploring for his return. I can't see her face because of the multitude of umbrellas, but I hear the anguish in her voice. I wonder if she can imagine what lies ahead.

Kidnappings are cruel. They are part of the landscape in Colombia, perhaps less common now than a few years back when children were snatched from their schoolyards for ransom. But in kidnappings the family knows who is holding their relative. The motive may be economic or political, but there's usually a sense of a plan of action: get the money or pressure the government for humanitarian exchanges or some other demands. There's often a place: the victim is in the city or the plains or the mountains, and sometimes tangible evidence is provided of their well-being.

Forcible disappearances are beyond cruel. There is no sign of life or death or of the author or the motives. The person just vanishes. The posters strike a chord with me. Not long ago, I published a book about a disappeared Guatemalan journalist, Irma Flaquer, a valiant reporter who wrote a column "What Others Don't Dare Write."

There were no posters for Irma. No one dared. How sad it is that "disappear" has become part of our vocabulary, that *desaparecido* is shorthand for "forcibly disappeared." The grandmothers of the Plaza de Mayo in Argentina, mothers in Santiago de Chile, and women's groups throughout Latin America and elsewhere have made the word common, but its infinite cruelty cannot be described. Thirty years later, I listen to the agony of Irma's sister and son and daughter-in-law and grandson as they wonder what happened. There are no bones to mourn. There is no certainty.

As I listen to Jaime's daughter, I wonder if she too will be looking for a body thirty years from now.

The small group of workers, students, and activists at the rally march toward the Plaza de Bolívar. The rain is imminent, and I decide to go home. In the plaza, the protesters will light candles for Jaime's return.

I have just come back from the plaza on my way home from lunch. I know that a huge banner, a replica of the posters, is hanging over the city hall, taking up one whole side of the plaza.

The text on the banner is a bit different from that of the posters. On the lampposts and the walls and the storefronts, the posters call citizens to the rally and march.

The banner starts out the same, "Aparezca Jaime," but underneath it explains: "The only thing that ought to disappear is fear, poverty, inequality, and indifference—never people."

I watch the protesters straggle out of sight. I wonder if a few candles will make a difference.

POSTSCRIPT

The body of Jaime Gómez was found by the dog Osa María and her hiker owners on April 23, 2006, in a desolate mountainous section of the National Park. Authorities claimed his death was most likely a sports accident.

My neighbor, a professor at the National University, teaches Jaime's daughter in one of his classes. He reminds me that Diana came to Harvard to give a presentation about theatre a year ago. And then I remember that we sat and ate lunch together with a group of Colombians after the presentation on a Colombian version of "Here Was Troy."

Jaime Gómez left our building after a work session with Piedad Córdoba at 11 p.m. the night before his disappearance, the doorman now tells us. I'm still not sure if I had ever seen Jaime in the elevator. I only know that I will never, never see him again.

Good Friday: The Passion

Yoga class is early morning on Fridays. I scrambled into my gym clothes and athletic shoes. It was only then that I remembered that it was Good Friday. Well, no one had said there was no class Good Friday. I might as well go see. Then I'd come back and change and head off to church somewhere.

Yoga is only a few blocks from my house, on the top floor of a parking garage. Stores and restaurants are often still closed when I leave the house. This time, even the parking garage was closed.

I had forgotten what Good Friday was like in Bogotá. I visit frequently over Christmas and had watched that holiday evolve from a time of religious celebrations when the city shut down for a month to a season of shopping frenzy and shorter vacations. I was unconsciously expecting the same.

The coffee shop down the street was one of the few places open, and I decided to indulge in breakfast. I ordered a glass of freshly squeezed juice; a cup of coffee; and a *tamal*, the corn-mass Colombian delight of pork and chicken and garbanzo beans, like a palm-leaf-wrapped surprise package. There was no hot sauce, and the fresh juice was too sweet. I'm not a breakfast eater, even though I like breakfast food. I drank the coffee, picked at the *tamal*. The restaurant was hopping.

When I emerged from the restaurant out onto the Séptima, the city had come to life. People dressed no better than I were flooding into the Mass at the sixteenth-century Las Nieves church, and I decided to follow. A Mass was going on, but families with children in tow were circulating about the church, stopping by colonial statues depicting Christ's passion.

The Séptima was closed to traffic, just as it is on Sundays, but instead of the hordes of bikes and skaters taking advantage of the wide avenue, families were strolling. The word *romería* sprung into my head. These folks were roaming from church to church and headed up to Monserrate, the white shrine overlooking Bogotá. I followed.

I stopped in at Las Aguas church and sat for a minute, collecting my thoughts about Good Friday, the passion before the resurrection. I strolled past the Universidad de los Andes and watched the crowd becoming denser and denser. Some people were already coming down from the shrine, clutching bottles of water and long plastic packages of typical Colombian cookies and crackers like *achiras*.

Up the way, it seemed like a carnival on either side of the road. People were hawking every imaginable variety of fried meat and sausage, salty baked potatoes and sweet fried plantains, cookies and crackers, water and soft drinks, white T-shirts for church, pirated movies and CDs, fruit salad, and earrings. Silver-painted mimes lined the road, as still as statues until you dropped money in their cups. Then they acknowledged their humanity by moving and smiling.

A rock band played. Highly inappropriate, I thought, until I realized that it was a Christian rock band, singing "Calvario a Morir"—"Calvary to Die"—to a hard-rock beat. Practically every store and parking lot displayed a sign, "Baños—$500," bathrooms that were open to the roaming public for five hundred pesos—twenty-five cents or so.

I make my way up the mountain. The sun is strong, and I am

beginning to feel the altitude. Bogotá is at an elevation of 2,600 meters, about a mile and a half above sea level. That altitude has never bothered me, but Monserrate is 3,160 meters high, nearly two miles. I'm well on the way to the top. The crowd forms a bottleneck. I remember my dictionary definition of *romería*. It's a pilgrimage. This is too crowded a pilgrimage for me; it seems as if the entire city is roaming up to the mountaintop shrine.

I start down again. The rock band is still playing, prefacing a new tune with "Pedimos paz para este país que tanto la necesita" (Let's pray for peace for this country that so needs it). I buy water from a hawker who is selling it in bags and bottles. I have a thousand-peso bill since I spent the little I had taken with me on breakfast earlier. "Alcanza?" I ask him—do I have enough for a bottle? He sells me a bottle.

I sit and begin to listen to the peace message of the band, trying to open the bottle. I ask one of the hawkers for help in twisting off the cap. "That's 1,200," he says. "She already paid for it," the other hawker intervenes. It is only then that I realize that he gave me a break.

Refreshed, I pick up my pace and walk down the steep road. Hordes of people are walking up. The vendors are doing a brisk business. A middle-aged man with a mustache hurls a toy parachute with a green-camouflaged soldier up into the air. I can't see if the soldier has a gun. The parachute drifts toward the ground.

"Buy one," shouts the man in a vendor's booming voice, "para la alegría de los niños"—for your kids' happiness. The rock band keeps singing about peace.

Books

A security guard is reading a book, mouthing the words with difficulty as if he were an unpracticed reader. Crowds swirl around the thirty-something guard, lost in his private world of reading. The visitors to the Nineteenth Bogotá International Book Fair are searching for books of their own, rushing to events, spotting authors. I seem to be the only one who is intrigued by the guard. I approach him, but he doesn't look up. I glimpse at the book. I am surprised to see that the author is Italian writer Italo Calvino.

I guess I had been expecting to see a mystery novel or a romance. But then again, I shouldn't be surprised by the reading habits of *bogotanos*. The book fair is packed, even though it charges admission. Teachers and librarians crowd into workshops on such topics as how to read art books with children or how to get more funding for public libraries. Couples parade together; families tow their children along; the book fair is bustling with author signings and cultural events. A festival atmosphere predominates.

Bogotá is a democratic city, it seems to me, when it comes to books. The library system extends into the poorest neighborhoods. These libraries are not the shabby, ramshackle affairs with torn volumes that one often associates with poor urban neighborhoods. Instead, they are designed by Colombia's best architects and packed with the latest books and computer services.

The citywide rapid bus service offers free books at certain stations. The system's called Libros al Viento (Books in the Wind). The books themselves range from Leon Tolstoy and Edgar Allen Poe to the Grimm Brothers and Oscar Wilde, plus a wide selection of Colombian authors such as Héctor Abad, Antonio García, Juan Manuel Roca, and Lina María Pérez.

Bus riders take a book, and when they have finished, they can return it and take another. One out of three riders actually does return the books, but according to an in-depth study by the Bogotá Institute of Culture and Tourism, four out of five riders recognize that "uno de sus objetivos [es] el fomento de la solidaridad y la cultura ciudadana, a través del estímulo a la circulación de un bien público" (one of the objectives is to foment solidarity and the culture of citizenship by promoting books as a public good). In March of this year, according to the same study, twenty titles— and a total of 178,396 books—had been distributed.

The study had some interesting things to say about the almost 200,000 free TransMilenio books circulating throughout the city. Fourteen percent of the riders read the books with their family, and 8.6 percent read the books to their kids. Four percent read the books together with friends, and a hefty 31 percent loaned the book to people they knew, friends or neighbors. I think of the security guard and his book and wonder if book reading might spread like a virus, of the positive type, that is.

Beyond the book fairs and the free book dispensers in the bus stations, the tongue twister of Paraderos Paralibros Paraparques — Book Stops in the Parks — are mobile book stands in thirty-three parks throughout the city.

Bogotá has always been a city of bookstores. It's also been a city with a wide assortment of pirated books at reasonable prices, an unfortunate demonstration of this city's reading habit. Bogotá is making reading a habit.

So I wasn't surprised when I picked up the informational flyer at the book fair. Bogotá is joining the ranks of Madrid; Alexandria, Greece; New Delhi; Montreal; Turin, Italy; and Amberes, Belgium. Next year it will become the Capital Mundial del Libro 2007 — the World Capital of the Book.

Gabo

I may be the only person in the world who has offended Gabriel García Márquez, not once, but twice.

Maybe I should clarify first that I'm a fan of García Márquez, or Gabo, as he is affectionately known by the Colombian public. The public shows its affection by buying his books, both in the bookstores and in pirated editions. In fact, so many pirated editions are sold even before the books appear in the stores that

García Márquez changed the ending in his last book just before it went to press to stymie the counterfeiters.

García Márquez' presence is felt in spirit at the well-attended International Book Fair. Gabo's books are here, but so is the love for reading that having a Nobel Prize winner seems to have instilled in the population. A poll has found that Colombians on average read only one book a year, but I think that reading—like Gabo—is a positive value in the public imagination in a way that it is not in other Latin American countries.

And reading is probably on the increase. Public libraries are an integral part of the city landscape. At the 2003 inauguration of the $10 million Tintal Library in a poor neighborhood, former Bogotá mayor Antanas Mockus observed, "Here there is a conflict that the protagonists say is caused by social injustice. Public projects like these generate equality. The books are arms that open the way."

Schoolchildren crowd the halls at the book fair, held every year in Bogotá's sprawling Corferias, almost twice the size of a U.S. football field. Journalism students, intellectuals, book lovers, and people with tired feet pack into a panel on the challenges for journalism. *Gatopardo* magazine editor Fernando Gómez talks about an issue for which he asked writers to do interviews with an author they have always wanted to meet.

My mind drifts to García Márquez. Back in 1981, I was working with *Time* as a Bogotá correspondent. The magazine was doing a special feature on what famous intellectuals thought about the war in Central America and assigned me an interview with García Márquez. He had recently been awarded the French Legion of Honor, the highest award that culture-obsessed European country gives to a foreigner.

I got Gabo's telephone number from a literary critic friend and called. He agreed to the interview and even sent a chauffeur in a Volkswagen to pick me up from my downtown apartment. His residence was tucked closer to the mountains in what was then quite the northern part of Bogotá. The city has drifted northward now, but then it seemed a long way away, a tranquil and leafy neighborhood.

His apartment was filled with books and modern art, and his wife, Mercedes, offered me the ubiquitous Colombian *tinto*, a strong shot of coffee in a tiny cup. I pulled out my tape recorder, placing it on the large glass coffee table, and asked Gabo my question about Central America. "The Americas are like a ship," the author told me. "Some go first class, some go second class, and others are in stowage. But if the ship sinks, all of us are going to go down together. That's why Central America is important."

It was a lovely sound bite, and I had the feeling that Gabo was about to call the chauffeur and have him take me back downtown. But I had my *tinto* in front of me, an excuse to linger. I began to probe. I had travelled to Central America frequently for the *National Catholic Reporter* and *Time*. Indeed, it was my other world, my journalistic home away from Bogotá, a world of hopeful revolutions and brutal wars.

Gabo—who in addition to being a novelist is an excellent journalist—caught on that I was a good source of information. Neither he nor I had declared the interview over, so I kept the tape recorder running, replacing the cassette as the tape ran out. We talked about the individual countries in Central America, its literary traditions, U.S. policy, the Colombian situation. The cassettes ran out; I wished I had brought more than two.

He gave me a tour of his white-walled duplex apartment, showing me his artwork and study space and electric typewriter. There were scheduled blackouts in Colombia back then to conserve electricity, and he complained that they were programmed precisely during his most productive work times. He pulled books off his shelf and commented on some of his favorite tomes. After three hours, he sent me on my way downtown.

Time had asked me for his opinions on Central America, so I transcribed the parts of the tape that had to do with that region and added in a little color about his apartment and the interview. The newsweeklies have reporters in the field send material, and then writers in New York craft the story. The feature was scheduled to come out in two weeks.

But then there was a crisis in the Mideast, and the story was postponed for a week. The next week, Prince Charles and Princess Di were married in England, and the story on Central America was once again postponed.

On March 27, 1981, García Márquez sought asylum at the Mexican Embassy in Bogotá, after a warning that the Colombian military had accused him of conspiring with guerrillas.

An editor from *Time* called me with an urgent request. That the author of *One Hundred Years of Solitude* was fleeing his homeland was big news. Did I have anything else from the interview? He asked me to write a file with everything from the interview, including physical descriptions of the apartment. I emptied my notebook, describing the white sofa and walls, the artwork, his comment about the blackouts, his relationship with Mercedes, his remarks about Colombia. I made no attempt to edit: the story would be written in New York.

On March 30, President Ronald Reagan was shot by a lone gunman in Washington. The assassination attempt sent shock waves around the United States, compounded by the vivid memories of the death of President John F. Kennedy. The García Márquez story wouldn't run: the magazine needed the space for the Reagan events. However, the editor had a proposal. *People*, which belonged to Time Inc., was interested in the story, if I was willing for him to turn over the files. "Sure," I said, not wanting to see either my work or the interview go entirely to waste.

The 604-word *People* story quoted Gabriel García Márquez as telling a reporter in Mexico, "I've never wielded any weapon but my typewriter," after his hasty departure from Colombia. The typewriter reference apparently sparked the writer's imagination. He wrote that Gabriel García Márquez had sought asylum in Mexico, saying that his life was in danger because of the army accusations. However, the writer said, some of his close friends in Bogotá had said that he had left because he was fed up with blackouts that put his electric typewriter out of commission during his peak writing hours.

That was all that was left of my three-hour interview with García Márquez. I wanted to crawl into a hole and never come out again. Bernie Diederich, the Mexico City bureau chief at the time, went to see García Márquez to apologize. Gabo said he understood the way the press worked well enough and that he knew it wasn't my fault. He graciously accepted the apology.

The next year he won the Nobel Prize.

Fast forward sixteen years. I am giving a short talk in Los Angeles at the Inter American Press Association meeting on my investigations into the case of disappeared Guatemalan journalist Irma Flaquer. Gabriel García Márquez is in the audience; he is giving the keynote speech, titled "El Mejor Oficio del Mundo," "The Best Job in the World"—namely, journalism.

In introductory remarks, he mentions something about his homes in Spain and Mexico. Although he maintains an apartment in Bogotá, he is not there very frequently. He's said to have places in Cartagena and in Barranquilla, on Colombia's Caribbean coast, as well as in Cuernavaca, Barcelona, Paris, and Havana.

His speech is absolutely inspirational, recalling the days when journalists didn't go to school and met for hours to talk about current events and their stories.

During the break, I wait for the elevator to my room. Gabo gets into the elevator. I am alone with Gabo in an elevator. I hope he doesn't remember me from the *People* story. It's sixteen years later and a completely different context. I hope he will say something about my little talk, maybe something about the world's disappeared. Anything. There is silence. I hate silence in elevators.

I compliment him on his speech. He grunts a smile but doesn't say anything more. I've always been curious about how one maintains multiple homes. I have my heart in many different places but have never been able to figure out the logistics of maintaining two homes, let alone several. So I ask him how he manages it.

He hears my question in an entirely different way. I sense anger and annoyance in his voice. Somehow he perceives me to be saying that he can't have much class consciousness or solidarity with the poor if he lives like a rich man. He is defensive, and we are in an elevator.

The elevator thankfully gets to my floor, and I say a polite good-bye. I can't remember if he answered or not. If I get to see him again, I'd like to tell him that his literature has a lot to do with Bogotá's being named the World Capital of the Book for 2007. I'd like to tell him that I teach his speech from Los Angeles to my journalism students. But mainly I'd like not to offend him.

Santa Marta: Listening to Students

Journalism students often bury their leads. That's reporter's jargon for not putting the important facts, the real news, first. As I teach a workshop to communications students in Santa Marta on the Caribbean coast, I sometimes wonder if they are burying their leads or whether the world just seems different—the war as perpetual backdrop.

During the first class, I assign students to interview each other about the scariest experiences in their lives. One story, entitled "Restless Childhood," recounts in great detail how a sister bribed her little brother to go into a well, then panicked when her brother closed the top of the well. The story has a happy ending, since the parents witnessed the scene, and the only calamity was that the girl was scolded in public.

It's the kind of story I get from my students in the United States, except the water is usually a swimming pool instead of a well. But then the student's story shifts:

Everything began at 8 in the morning on September 25, 2000, when the telephone rang and a trembling voice said that [my father] had been kidnapped by the rebel group FARC.

There were moments of panic, now at home, this time not child's mischief, but the cruelty of assassins, but it was not all over. At 11 a.m. something even worse happened, another call, in which a man identifying himself as a guerrilla from Front 19 of the FARC declared that [my father] had been murdered, and if we didn't believe it, we could look on the outskirts of the city, where the body had been tossed in a black plastic bag.

Like the story of the boy in the well, this tale also has a happy ending. After three weeks, the father walked through the door, dirty, disheveled, and with tears in his eyes—very much alive. The student, who is now twenty, tells her interview partner that she is trying to forget *los duros momentos*, the tough moments.

I look at the students in my class. They are little more than teenagers. They wear jeans and T-shirts with brand names and slogans; the girls wear long dangly earrings and high heels. They could be kids in Boston or Buenos Aires. Occasionally one of them snaps a piece of gum, and another lets a cell phone ring with the tune of "Jingle Bells."

They continue to read their interviews out loud. A second story is entitled "El secuestro: Vivir para sufrirlo" (Kidnapping: Experience it to suffer it), wordplay on the title of Gabriel García Marquez' memoir. The twenty-year-old student recounts the kidnapping of her great-grandmother, writing in Spanish about "a great scar" and noting that "although it is healing with the passage of time, the marks it left on her life will always be present."

Workers on the great-grandmother's farm told the family that paramilitary men showed up on the property in the middle of the morning as the ninety-four-year-old woman was setting out to collect some hen eggs. On the eighth day, the great-grandmother was returned to exactly the same spot from which she had been taken. Her body was bruised, and she showed signs of being beaten, although she claimed that she had been treated well and that she had had enough to eat.

And like the student whose father nearly died at the hands of guerrillas, this student ends up with a fervent desire to erase it all from her memory: "Today I'm in my sixth semester and living the life of any ordinary young woman university student, but at times the images of the incident arise in my mind. I would like to erase them in a definitive way, but I know that as much as I try, I will never be able to do so."

Another student had a cousin kidnapped; he doesn't say by what group. The event left the student with a fear of physical mistreatment and suffering.

Yet another student remembers a telephone call received during a light dinner of fruits and cereal: "You have 24 hours to get out or die." She didn't specify the group.

The students tell me that Santa Marta is under control now, that the paramilitary forces have cleaned up the market and violence is basically not visible because it is repressed. They seem grateful, and I don't comment.

Violence may be past, or it may be on hold, but it is a more recent memory than in Bogotá, a more visible wound. I return to my five-star hotel, where the university has lodged me, and change into my bathing suit. I walk along the white sand, the blue-green salty water lapping at my toes, the sun warming my chilled Bogotá bones.

The frightening horror of my students' stories, set in places so very near, now feel very, very distant. In the hot tropical sun, the war has once again become invisible.

The Strike

Bogotá woke up in silence. The mountain air drifting into my bedroom window was clean and fresh, with a touch of pine and eucalyptus.

I was startled when I went out and found myself in a traffic jam. The buses of the city were on strike, the huge buses, the small *busetas*, and the tiny *colectivos* that belch their way through the city. The government had lifted *pico y placa*, the measure that restricts automobiles from circulating during certain hours and days of the week, in accordance with license plate numbers.

More cars than usual were on the street, but for the most part they weren't honking and spewing black smoke. The only buses were those in the TransMilenio system, and it was their existence that had sparked the strike. The government wanted the ordinary buses to keep away from the TransMilenio routes and to keep out of certain neighborhoods during peak hours for environmental reasons. Bus owners said, "Nothing doing," and called a *paro*.

I remembered strikes from the 1970s and 1980s, usually for an increase in bus fare. Lots of folks stayed home from work, taking the opportunity for a day of leisure. Fewer people had cars then, and the TransMilenio wasn't even a dream.

But it now appeared that everyone in the city was out, determined to have life as usual. Lines and lines snaked around the station for the TransMilenio, and the system even ran out of tickets. People were riding bicycles and motorcycles and horse-drawn carts converted into taxis to transport residents of the city's poorer neighborhoods. Private cars mounted destination signs on their windshields and picked up passengers for a small fee. And people were walking everywhere.

Mayor Luis Eduardo Garzón ordered public schools to close and encouraged private schools to do the same. This mandate took some of the burden off of parents to get their children to and from school. Universities canceled classes. But for the most part the city refused to be paralyzed.

Friendly camaraderie prevailed yet was missing the spontaneous enjoyment and solidarity of a New England snowstorm or a New York transit strike. A mood of apprehension lingered in the air, as people tried to go about their business. In the middle of an election campaign with a labor leader leftist mayor and a rightist "law and order" president, a bus strike was a recipe for trouble and a long, long battle.

"It was a transportation strike that made Jorge Eliécer Gaitán step down from the mayor's office," warned Doña Inés, a longtime friend in her eighties that I go to visit weekly. "Transportation strikes are very serious." She recalled that in the 1940s the populist mayor had wanted all transportation workers to wear uniforms (there was a streetcar, as well as buses at the time). Instead, they went out on strike. I didn't know that bit of history, just that Gaitán's assassination in 1948 had sparked a period of political violence.

The residents in Doña Inés' *hogar del abuelo*—senior citizen residence—pass their time watching television. Now the nurses and the attendants couldn't keep their eyes off the TV. Many of them had walked long distances to work, and one of them was limping from her blistered feet. After the visit, I stopped by the Galerías shopping center. Shoppers and passersby stood around looking at public televisions hung from the ceiling in shopping center corridors. President Uribe was saying that he would support the mayor. In Bogotá one can often judge the seriousness of an event by the number of people watching television in public spaces. There were a lot of people watching.

Bus strike leaders were saying that the strike would continue indefinitely. The mayor was saying that he wouldn't give in to pressure. Former labor leader or not, Garzón said the strike was blackmail. A May 3 editorial in *El Tiempo* called the strike "an abusive protest" and an *"enorme trauma"*—a huge trauma. It was only then that I began to understand what I had only intuited. Normality in Bogotá lingers on the surface; people crave normality, and they were determined to carve order out of chaos.

And order somehow swiftly did emerge from chaos. Mayor Garzón kept emphasizing that this was a bus owners' strike and not a labor strike. He would not negotiate until the city's 20,847 buses, *busetas*, and *colectivos* were back on the road. President Uribe kept on saying he would support the mayor but did not give any recipes (at least not in public) for what the mayor should do.

At the end of the second day of the strike, the bus owners called a halt to the *paro* and said they would negotiate. I woke up the next morning to honking bus horns and the smell of diesel. I've never been so glad.

The first thing that Carlos Santacruz asked was, "You don't have any restrictions on where you can travel, do you?" The dynamic director of a nongovernmental organization called ASOPATIA was arranging my trip to a community project, a couple of hours north of Pasto.

"ASOPATIA" stands for Asociación Supradepartamental de Municipios de la Región de Alto Patia, an acronym that basically means an association of small towns in the High Patia region north of Pasto, a coca-growing area that has been plagued by poverty, environmental degradation, and conflict among irregular armed forces that often finds peasants caught in the middle.

I had met Santacruz at a session of community groups organized at my request at the Mariana University, where I was teaching journalism workshops. I'm breaking my own rules, not anyone else's restrictions, by going to Remolinos. As a journalist in the 1970s and 1980s here in Colombia, I used to go looking for the war throughout the country, but, all too often, in Bogotá the war would come to me. The Left was being mowed down, embassies were being taken over, and bombs sometimes exploded. Daily life was still enjoyable and routine, but urban violence was more on the surface in Bogotá than it is now.

I see the displaced people on the street, a constant reminder of the domestic conflict. When I receive invitations to teach in other cities, I accept. After all, I'm being invited as a Fulbright scholar who lives in Bogotá, so visiting other cities makes up part of my ongoing quest to understand "daily life."

This time, I'm stretching a little farther in an attempt to see "reality," where the displaced come from, what the war feels like "out there." I wake up one morning, dreaming that I have been sent out to cover a battle between guerrillas and paramilitary forces in a town I cannot find. I decide to, at least a little bit, go looking.

The trip along the Pan-American Highway, in the company of ASOPATIA representatives and a professor from the Mariana University, is a virtual tour of much of what afflicts Colombia today. Up in the surrounding mountains, down in the valleys, are small towns that have recently been fumigated to wipe out coca leaves. That's not all that's been wiped out. So have small plots of self-sustaining agriculture, fruits, and vegetables. The richer farmers move their coca plants elsewhere, I am told; the poorer ones move to the city or go hungry.

Here is deforestation. Here is poverty. The talk turns to begging and robbery on the highway. The begging has almost been eliminated because of an ASOPATIA project. The robberies have subsided, I'm told, at least during the day.

We end up in a church in Remolinos, where community representatives have come from far and wide. They look like U.S. cowboys with big straw hats and bronzed faces. The meeting is a preliminary one to determine what kind of projects outlying communities want. ASOPATIA emphasizes the organization and development of citizen participation, and the community representatives are here to voice their priorities for European Community funding. There's only one hitch. The European Community does not fund infrastructure, but these citizens want bridges and roads to get their products to market. The discussion goes on and on.

The church is unbearably hot. Remolinos is at least 15 degrees Fahrenheit hotter than Pasto. The sound system is muffled, and the discussion often hard to understand. Liza, the professor, and I decide to take a break and look for bottled water. We are both perspiring profusely,

At the local gas station, which is out of water, a woman attendant questions us in a friendly and probing manner. She's heard there's a meeting in the church from all over. Who's there? How many? What are they talking about? I think that perhaps I am overreacting. Colombians like to ask questions that most U.S.

folk would consider impertinent. But Liza, who is from Bogotá, shares my concern. We give vague answers and move on to look for water to quench our thirst. A paramilitary spy? A guerrilla collaborator? Or someone who is just trying to figure out how many customers she may have later in the day? Here too, the war is invisible but always present. Here too, one just doesn't know.

We find our water and go back to the church.

Afterwards, during a long lunch of fish, rice and plantains, we learn about the importance of sustainable agriculture and soil recovery for the region. Some of the politics of the region is also explained. Indigenous groups in the Cauca Department (state) are quite militant, but their governor is an archconservative. In Nariño Department, the peasants are generally conservative, but the governor is a leftist. ASOPATIA covers both departments, and the contradictions make for unusual alliances.

We head back toward Pasto. On the way, unannounced, we stop at the little village of Manzano. A strong waft of fresh bread greets us. We pull up to a small storefront with a huge baking oven. A group of teenaged girls and a slightly older male baker are cutting up bread. They used to be beggars on the Pan-American Highway, we are told, but now they earn their living baking bread and making peanut products. What impresses me is that ours is an unplanned visit, but the bakers are absolutely and spontaneously eloquent in explaining their projects.

ASOPATIA may have helped the youth organize, but the project is theirs. The involvement of children has led to parental participation, and ASOPATIA estimates that all the families in Manzano now have self-sustaining vegetable plots. The percentage of children attending school has risen from 45 percent to 95 percent, we are told. I can't verify the figures, but I felt the enormous pride and dignity of these young people. I tasted the fresh-baked bread and wished that some of it had been served at my hotel in Pasto.

As we passed once again by the bottoms of the mountains of the fumigated villages, I wondered out loud whether the Manzano project could be duplicated. No two villages are alike, my interlocutors told me, and each must find its own path to peace and development. Still, with the taste of the fresh-baked bread in my mouth and the memory of the debating peasants in the church, I felt hope.

Two months have passed since my trip to Remolinos. The presidential elections are approaching. I hear on the radio that along the Pan-American Highway, indigenous people are protesting President Uribe's reelection and the Free Trade Agreement with the United States. I think of Cauca, where native peoples are well organized and dedicated to unarmed resistance. The reports say that an indigenous man has been killed, and 32 protesters have been seriously wounded.

The road that connects Cauca with Ecuador is blocked. That means Remolinos and Manzano. That means the kids with the bread and the community leaders with their cowboy hats and even the inquisitive woman at the gas station.

In Nariño Department, protesters are coca farmers, rather than indigenous groups, who obstructed the highway. Their numbers were estimated at ten thousand. Radio news reports capture helicopters buzzing overhead. Coca growers admit to the press that they have received some pressures from the guerrillas—and even from the paramilitary—to protest. Nevertheless, they say, recent fumigations have done away with their livelihood. This is not a forced protest.

On May 18, according to human rights groups, tanks began to approach Remolinos. Machine guns were fired from helicopters, and people fled toward the school and other refuges. Military and police beat up protesters, including women and children, and fired tear gas into the midst of the demonstration. Agricultural plots and personal property were burned by the troops, according to the reports. Even those who had sought safety were not safe. Human rights activists, reporting from the scene, claimed that men, women, and children seeking refuge in the school were forced out of the building and beaten, and many of their belongings burned by antiriot troops.

Injuries were many: fractures from beatings and wounds caused by shooting from the helicopter and other gunfire. The wounded were sent to the local hospital, but there weren't enough doctors, paramedics, and medicine to take care of them. An RCN national radio reporter was detained while covering the military actions but was released a few hours later.

Members of the national police were reported to continue to search for "subversives" at the exits to Remolinos and another nearby town, Policarpa. Paramilitary forces controlled a highway bridge.

Carlos Maya, Nariño's human rights advocate, which is a government post (*defensor del pueblo de Nariño*), broadcast a warning on the radio about the region's "grave humanitarian crisis."

In the city of Pasto, he said, four thousand people had fled from the Remolinos area, adding to the some twenty thousand war refugees that already call that city their home.

Social action, he stressed, should not face "police and military repression as a response, but should resort to dialogue and a humanitarian spirit, and hope that someday, the directives of reason will win out."

ASOPATIA director Carlos Santacruz has come to Bogotá for a meeting with the national network of peace associations. He tells me that twenty-two people from the Remolinos area have been killed as a result of the demonstrations. Paramilitary forces are continuing to murder participants who return from Pasto to their home communities, and he fears the situation might continue or even escalate. The Manzano project suspended activities for a while, but now the project is back in action, he tells me. There is a note of sadness and exhaustion in his voice.

A few days later, *El Tiempo* reports even more violence, as paramilitary troops single out activists and coca workers. In the Patía River, another five bodies were found floating, some of them mutilated. Official sources were quoted as saying that the murders were in retaliation for the coca growers' march on the Pan-American Highway to protest fumigations.

It has been a little over two months since Carlos Santacruz asked me if I had any prohibitions on travel, a short while since that uneventful trip down the Pan-American Highway. I can still imagine the taste of the fresh-baked bread in my mouth, the elusive taste of hope and peace.

Abortion and Citizens' Rights

"Women in Colombia experienced a victory today," I first wrote on May 10, 2006. I've been fretting over that choice of words ever since. From my point of view, women did win a victory with the partial lifting of the abortion ban. But I'm modifying that for now to "women's rights activists" because abortion has become a hot election issue, and women are among its fiercest opponents.

On May 10 the Constitutional Court declared that women have the right to abortion if the case is one of rape or incest, if the mother's life or health is at risk, or if the fetus is deformed.

The decision is a long way from *Roe v. Wade*, the 1973 U.S. Supreme Court decision that guarantees women the right to abortion during the first trimester of pregnancy, overturning all state laws restricting or prohibiting abortion. Women in Colombia can still go to jail for a year and a half to five years for having an abortion, except in cases involving the specific exceptions.

Yet, in a country where the Catholic Church is extremely powerful, the decision is both important and courageous. It's not that abortion doesn't occur in Colombia. Middle- and upper-class women go quietly to their medical doctors to deal with unwanted pregnancies. Poor women go to clandestine "butchers" and often end up in a hospital emergency room—or dead—from complications.

According to Colombia's Social Welfare Ministry, about one in three illegal abortions results in complications that threaten women's health and lives. The ministry reports that abortion is the third-ranking cause of maternal mortality, responsible for 17 percent of such deaths.

A little more than two years ago, a working-class woman suffering from cancer was forced to bear her child. Marta González, a single mother of three, had been diagnosed with uterine cancer while pregnant with her fourth child. She needed to stop chemotherapy and radiation during her pregnancy, and the cancer rapidly spread through her body. There was no way she could obtain a legal abortion. She told her story to the newspapers because she knew that her two toddlers and her seventeen-year-old daughter would soon be orphaned. The new court decision will cover cases like hers, although women will need doctor's certification to obtain an abortion. It remains to be seen whether doctors will be willing to cite the "mental health" category of the "risk to health" clause to help women with too little money and too many children.

The Constitutional Court debated the measure on two consecutive days, for eleven hours each day. For months now, right-to-life groups and the Catholic Church have mobilized protests, including controversial mass protests by children not old enough to know what the word "abortion" means. Opponents see the decision as somewhat like legalizing murder, and Cardinal Alfonso López Trujillo called the decision "an attack on human life."

The case was brought to court a year ago by lawyer Mónica Roa, exercising her citizen's right to grievance known as *tutela*, a guarantee of fundamental rights spelled out in Colombia's progressive 1991 Constitution. The case was thrown out for technical reasons just before Christmas of 2005, but Roa persisted despite growing public opposition. And although in her original *tutela* she had called for decriminalization of abortion for the reasons spelled out above, in her second *tutela* she upped the ante. Women have a right to abortion, period.

She obtained what she had asked for in the first petition. Roa, speaking to journalists, called the decision "historic" and said that, at least for now, she will not insist on full abortion rights.

Even beyond the partial victory for abortion rights advocates, the case came to the court as an exercise in citizens' rights, significant in a country in which power often weighs more heavily than justice. Last year, for example, a pregnant sergeant employed a *tutela* to keep the army from retiring her from active duty. The Constitutional Court found in her favor. Citizens constantly use *tutelas* to obtain advanced health care or medicines not routinely provided under Colombia's public medical system.

In 1996 a group of peasants were chased off their land on the Atlantic coast by a well-armed paramilitary group and were threatened with a massacre if they returned. The head of the paramilitary group was arrested on charges of terrorism, but the local prosecutor freed him, saying that threats were not "terrorism." The peasants eventually filed a *tutela* to protest faulty justice. They won. The Constitutional Court declared in 2003 that they were right: "Clearly, it is not necessary to set off bombs or provoke massacres to produce constant anxiety or terror."

In *El Tiempo* today, May 11, right under the article about the abortion decision, is another case of *tutela*. Magaly, a fifty-one-year-old transsexual who fathered five children and still lives with the children's mother, is demanding her right not to be refused a construction job on the grounds of sexual discrimination. She was turned away from the job after the prospective employer discovered that she had once been a man.

One of the reasons for the popularity of the *tutela* is that the 1991 Constitution defines fundamental rights in a very broad fashion, including the equality of rights and opportunities between the sexes; children's rights; senior citizen rights; rights for the handicapped; the right to health care, a clean environment, and a life with dignity; the right to recreation and sports; the right to private property and the social purpose this fulfils; the right to education; and the collective and individual rights of workers.

Most likely, when Colombians decide to extend abortion to the concept of a women's right to decide, that too will be accomplished through a *tutela*. The present abortion decision was a victory not only for women but also for citizens' rights.

Men don't whistle at me anymore on the Bogotá streets.

I'd forgotten about the long-ago wolf whistles and catcalls. But recently I was strolling down the Séptima right near my house, and an elderly man with disheveled hair and a slightly crazed air looked at me and said, "An angel in a skirt, finally a woman wearing a skirt." I do like to wear skirts, but at my last informal census, 93 out of 100 women here wear pants. So I wasn't quite sure if the gentleman in question was making a sociological assertion or a *piropo*, a flowery comment.

But the incident jogged my memory that in the 1970s and 1980s I could hardly walk down the street without comments, ranging from elegant to obscene, without being subjected to whistles and catcalls. Construction workers were the worst offenders, but basically the quality of the comment improved the higher the social class. I didn't like any of it.

My Colombian friends seemed to take the attention in stride, and some of them even said they enjoyed the comments, as long as they were decent. My gringa friends had all developed various tactics to confront the unwanted attention. One very tall and blonde acquaintance, a Nordic type, stared at the men and said, "So, where are we going?" They ran the other way.

I've been back in Colombia for months now, and the comment about my skirt was the first such remark I'd heard. What I wasn't sure of was whether I had changed or whether the city had. Did men still whistle at and make remarks to younger women? Or was that a thing of the past?

The memory of how uncomfortable I sometimes felt on Bogotá streets jolted me. I had mostly tried just to ignore the wolf whistles, a cultural difference perhaps, a manifestation of machismo, an affront to my gringa sense of privacy and feminism. I now wanted to find out if wolf whistling had gone the way of two-hour lunches. Bogotá, after all, has vested much pride and energy in its public spaces, and catcalls and other street harassment, at least in my opinion, infringed on women's enjoyment of that space.

Now, it's not to say that street harassment doesn't occur elsewhere. Forty years after the first wave of feminism in the United States, the New York–based Street Harassment Coalition started a blog dedicated to revealing the effects of what they see as an abundant problem that is widely treated as mundane. One poster writes that the problem permeates "the cultural and social landscape . . . which impacts our choices, our moods, our participation within and relationship to our communities." Street harassment is perhaps not so much a matter of culture as an assertion of power.

In a 1993 *Harvard Law Review* article, "Street Harassment and the Informal Ghettoization of Women," U.S. legal scholar Cynthia Grant Bowman theorizes:

> "[L]iberty," as John Locke observed, "is to be free from restraint and violence from others; which cannot be where there is no law. . . ." The liberty of women, in this most fundamental sense of freedom from restraint, is substantially limited by street harassment, which reduces their physical and geographical mobility and often prevents them from appearing alone in public places. In this sense, street harassment accomplishes an informal ghettoization of women—a ghettoization to the private sphere of hearth and home.
>
> The most fundamental definitions of liberty include the right of an individual to go where she chooses in spaces that are public. . . . In order to participate as equal citizens in the polis, women must reclaim the public space.

I'm not sure that any Colombian woman—or, for that matter, any resident gringa—has ever been kept off the streets by sucking sounds or wolf whistles. But in this capital city, where public space is a stated priority and where women are mayors, doctors, lawyers, police officials, army officers, and government ministers, I wonder if behavior has changed or if only my experience of it has changed.

Thus began my informal survey of female friends.

First, the gringas. I was surprised how unanimously they said they had been harassed on the street.

"I usually get hassled no matter how I'm dressed," said one twenty-five-year-old, three years younger than I was when I first came to Colombia. "It's usually pretty innocuous, sort of 'Hey, beautiful,' but if I get specific comments, it's on my butt."

"Construction workers are the worst, but I get it from everyone when I go running," said a student from Atlanta in her early twenties. "That's whistles and catcalls and sometimes a nice, 'Good luck, girl.'"

The general consensus seemed to be to ignore the comments, although a gringa or two said she would make some comment back.

I then continued my informal and highly unscientific survey among Colombian friends and acquaintances.

"They stopped whistling at me a long time ago," said a university professor in her thirties who likes to dress in baggy pants and sneakers. "And I think street harassment is actually less because workers don't sit on the street for hours anymore eating lunch and playing football. But it still happens, just not to me."

"Men often whistle, but it's mostly if they are standing around, not just walking on the street," said a twenty-eight-year-old political science student. "Then it's just looks."

Most agreed they got whistles and catcalls and flowery comments at least some of the time. There really did seem to be an invisible cutoff point, somewhere around age forty. But then I realized that these young women were in the same position as I am. I have no way of knowing if things have changed because men no longer whistle at me, and my respondents have no way to know if things have changed because most of them were toddlers or not born when men were whistling at me in the streets of Bogotá.

I asked a woman journalist friend in her mid-thirties the question, and I explained why I was asking it.

"I do get catcalls quite a bit," she said. "But then again, I do think Bogotá is modernizing. Construction workers used to be the worst offenders. But I now think they are embarrassed—*les da pena*—in mixed company. You see, lots of construction workers are women."

I don't miss the whistles at all.

Electing Álvaro

A slight woman in her twenties with a purple streak in her platinum hair stared at her finger, stained with indelible ink. Rosita had just voted for the first time.

I watched as voters, young, old, poor, rich, of all races and sartorial preferences, slinked around the electoral tables set up at Corferias, the oversized trade exhibition hall. The lines were long, but they moved fast and efficiently.

President Álvaro Uribe, because of a constitutional change the first president eligible for consecutive reelection for more than a century, had urged people to vote in celebration of democracy. The FARC had also urged people to vote—for anyone except Uribe—and promised not to keep citizens from going to the polls.

Most everyone agreed that this was an *elección anunciada*, a predetermined election, and that perhaps the only question was whether Uribe would win by enough in the first round for the presidency. He needed 50 percent, plus one vote.

Rosita was too young perhaps to remember what an *elección anunciada* really was. When I came to Bogotá in 1975 as a young journalist, the National Front was just ending. That was a rather odd system put into place after the ten-year period of violence that swept Colombia, whereby the two traditional parties—the Liberals and the Conservatives—alternated power.

Back then, I lived on Calle 19, a major downtown street, and it was closed off to host a series of polling stations right beneath my window. I held Election Day parties during the almost ten years I lived in Colombia, stocking up on beer and wine to compensate for "dry" elections and making a huge pot of corned beef for visitors. A variety of people always gathered at my apartment, from diplomats to theatre actors to business folk.

Election Day always felt like a party, both upstairs in my apartment and downstairs on the street. Yet the National Front cast very strong shadows during my first Colombian stay, and elections always seemed like an alternation of elites. When strong alternative candidates emerged, they were literally killed off. Fraud and vote buying were rampant. After I left, the situation got even worse, with leftist political forces decimated through the assassination of more than three thousand members of the legalized and once politically promising Patriotic Union.

Corferias—the fairgrounds where the voting tables from Calle 19 eventually moved—didn't feel as festive as the view from my window once did. Something was very different, a sort of earnestness, a feeling that one could make a difference by voting. I moved on from Corferias to a polling place in the northern part of the city, where a friend of mine was a voting monitor.

On my way up north, I passed numerous posters proclaiming "¡Adelante, Presidente!"—"Keep going, Mr. President!" Almost as frequent were signs for the leftist candidate Carlos Gaviria of the Alternative Democratic Pole, a jolly-looking, white-bearded university professor who was often dubbed "Papa Noel." The streets were quite empty. Policemen and the military patrolled. I didn't see anyone frisked, but the presence of security forces was heavy. Throughout the country, as I later read, more than 220,000 security forces were patrolling almost 10,000 polling stations.

I arrived at the polls where my friend had been assigned. Voters waited patiently in line at the entrance to vote and at the exit to have their finger painted with indelible ink. I watched as my friend checked *cédulas*—ID cards—and handed voters their ballots. Some four hundred people voted at her table, most of them for Uribe.

I tried to stay at the table while the votes were being counted, but was pleasantly told I had to leave. In any case, the vote tallies, my friend told me later, reflected the national count. Uribe captured 62 percent of the vote in Colombia, well above the 50 percent he needed to win in the first round. Carlos Gaviria came in second, with 22 percent, and Liberal Party candidate Horacio Serpa lagged behind, with less than 12 percent of the vote.

The day was still sunny and cool when the polls closed, so I decided to walk home, a marathon sixty-block walk. By the time I had got halfway, car horns had begun to honk and I could hear victorious shouts somewhere off in the distance. Uribe had won. The final count was not yet in, but it was now obvious that there would be no runoff.

I was surprised to learn that the voting abstention rate of more than 50 percent was as high as ever. Despite that figure, the elections seemed fresh and passionate.

Just days before, in Carlos Gaviria's closing campaign rally in the packed Plaza de Bolívar, I had stood amidst a sea of yellow T-shirts, the Polo Party color, and watched as raindrops fell and umbrellas came out and ralliers continued to chant. I had felt the energy of the chants—"El pueblo unido jamás será vencido," a traditional revolutionary slogan that asserts that a united people will never be defeated. Looking up, I had spotted soldiers on the nearby roofs of the Congress and the Palace of Justice. For a moment, I felt nervous. The rally went on without an incident.

How do I now explain what is so different when the outcome was what just about everyone expected?

Well, for one thing, the elections and most of the campaign were peaceful. A study by the Security and Democracy Foundation, a Bogotá think tank, indicated that campaign-season killings were down more than 75 percent from 2001–2002, the last electoral period, when the FARC kidnapped presidential candidate Ingrid Betancourt.

Election observers from the Organization of American States (OAS) monitored the voting process in a number of Colombian departments, witnessing the installation and opening of polling centers, the closing of the polls, and the vote count, as well as the transmission and publication of the results. The OAS announced on Election Day that its electoral observation mission had found that the Colombian vote took place "in an atmosphere of freedom, transparency and normalcy."

The observation mission noted that the Colombian election was marked by the "determination shown by voters who went to the polls in a clear demonstration of their commitment to democracy, particularly those who live in parts of the country that face serious security problems." That was something new and different in Colombia, where elections have been wracked by violence for years.

In addition, the strongest candidates were not from the traditional Liberal and Conservative parties, the parties whose visceral hatred sparked the ten-year bloodletting known as La Violencia. Uribe, originally a dissident liberal, has governed with a coalition of parties, many of them brand-new, but including the traditional conservatives. And Gaviria had run with a leftist party that was really a coalition of different groups. I think it's way too soon, as some pundits are doing, to predict that traditional parties are dead. Yet, the fact that one in five voters opted for the leftist alternative, and that no one was killed in the process, is an outcome far different from any that I have ever witnessed here before—or for that matter, that any Colombian in recent history has witnessed.

What's different also about these elections is that the top three candidates were technocrats, well connected with, but not necessarily a part of, Colombia's traditional political and economic elite. Serpa came from an impoverished background, and Gaviria's father had committed suicide when the candidate was a child. Uribe's father was a well-off landowner who had been killed twenty years ago by the FARC.

In U.S. terms, these are Clintons, not Kennedys or Bushes.

I finally reach my downtown apartment, not far from Uribe's campaign headquarters. I turn on the television to hear more election results. Reminiscing on today's events, I think of Rosita, the platinum- and purple-haired twenty-something at Corferias. And I realize that all day long I have been seeing enthusiastic young people, young people who worship the workaholic yoga-enthusiast president with his law-and-order agenda, and young people who have been working nonstop for their law professor idol Gaviria.

The abstention rate may be the same, but a new generation of voters has emerged. Television images confirm my intuition. Campaign headquarters are crowded with young folks, laughing, watching, waiting with their candidates. The television broad-caster is giving the latest results, with 93 percent of the vote in, and it's not quite dark yet.

The broadcaster's voice is drowned out by the raucous rattle of a helicopter. I look out my window. A Black Hawk is hovering outside in noisy vigil. Its dark silhouette makes a shadow against the green mountains.

Jamundí

The book-lined Bogotá studio of my novelist friend is quiet, filled with art and antiques. It's a peaceful setting for conversations, and our talk drifts from university politics to the friendly fire between po-lice officers and the military in the town of Jamundí the previous day, May 22, 2006. Ten members of an elite squad of antinarcot-ics police and their informant were shot to death.

The shootout took place in broad daylight on the grounds of a mental hospital. The whole event reminded me of *One Flew over the Cuckoo's Nest*, the movie with Jack Nicholson that shows men-tal patients to be saner than those that care for them. I mentioned the analogy to my friend, and he replied, "That was no friendly fire. Some narcos probably paid off the military to knock off the police."

That's why my friend's a novelist, I thought. Actually, I thought the suggested convoluted plot was worthy of a pretty bad novelist, which he is not. Friendly fire was bizarre enough, but an actual conspiracy was beyond belief.

I've never asked him if it was his novelist's mind at work or if he had some inside information. It turns out he was right.

The twenty-eight-man platoon, setting off a barrage of 150 bullets and seven grenades from roadside ditches and from behind bushes, knew exactly whom they were shooting at—fellow law officers, not left-wing guerrillas.

"You could hear the police shouting they had families and begging the soldiers not to shoot," said fifty-six-year-old Arcesio Morales in a newspaper interview. The psychiatric patient at Mi Casita—My Little Home—witnessed the twenty-eight-minute ambush from his hiding place in a ditch.

A week after the shootings, Attorney General Mario Iguarán declared in no uncertain terms, "This was not a mistake. It was a crime—a deliberate, criminal decision." He charged that the army was doing the bidding of drug traffickers. Forensic evidence showed that many of the members of the U.S.-trained police force were killed at point-blank range and that the informant was shot through the back of the head with just one bullet. In addition, the attorney general's office found cell-phone text messages indicating that the operation was carefully planned, according to newspaper reports.

A total of fifteen soldiers, including a colonel, are expected to face charges of aggravated homicide.

"What took place in Jamundí changes your thought process," Iguarán told reporters. "Previously I had the impression that the human rights abuses, if inevitable in every army throughout the world, weren't a real problem in Colombia. Now I have my doubts."

At least there wasn't a cover-up. President Uribe declared, "We are committed to transparency." But then no heads of higher-ups in the army have rolled.

Another trial of 147 soldiers is going on now. They allegedly stole millions of dollars from a guerrilla hideaway, proceeds from drugs trafficking and kidnap ransoms. During the trial, soldiers have testified that their superiors told them to return to look for more booty. I don't want to condone these soldiers, but it's certainly a crime I can understand. Poorly paid soldiers see an ill-earned fortune and decide to take it for their own. U.S. soldiers in Germany were not immune from looting; why should I expect more from a Colombian one?

Another army unit is being investigated for murdering peasants and then dressing the corpses as rebels to pass them off as guerrillas killed in battle. But then, this figures into the pressure to produce results, kind of a military production line. Again, I can't condone the actions, but I can understand how they arose.

The massacre at Jamundí touched me deeply, though, even from the time I protested the friendly fire to my novelist friend. The brutality and seeming irrationality of the incident were not only impossible to condone but morally impossible to understand. I am perfectly aware that the United Nations and human rights groups have asserted that Colombia's military is behind a recent wave of disappearances and killings of unarmed civilians. Government encouragement of head counts of dead guerrillas and rewards for capturing guerrilla leaders "dead or alive" do not exactly stimulate human rights.

Still, the army has developed credibility as an institution under President Álvaro Uribe and other recent administrations. The United States insisted on human rights compliance as part of its aid package. Whenever abuses occurred, Uribe dismissed a general or two (unlike in the Jamundí case thus far).

In my daily life, I see uniforms everywhere on the streets: army uniforms, police uniforms, presidential guard uniforms. My building is "militarized" because Senator Piedad Córdoba lives in the penthouse apartment. And when the doorman is busy, a soldier will politely open the door and greet me with a smile. Especially around election time, there was an armed soldier or a police officer on almost every corner. I've come to think of these guys as rural youths or guys from the barrio. They joke and chew gum and generally seem happy. At least in downtown Bogotá, when they ask for identification papers, they do it in a polite way (the higher the social class, the more polite the interaction, I noted).

I remember years ago watching police or military officers demand documents on the street. There was a *toque de queda* then, a curfew, and I remember being slightly afraid every time I went past a military man. I sometimes went out of my way a couple of blocks to avoid the Military Hospital near the Javeriana University.

Three years after I arrived in Bogotá in the *primera ronda*, President Julio César Turbay Ayala issued a "Security Statute" that granted greater authority and autonomy to the military. The 1978 decree identified new, vaguely defined crimes such as "disturbing public order," and it restricted press freedom. The statute was aimed at drug traffickers as well as the country's growing leftist rebels. Friends of mine who were involved with the progressive church and leading intellectuals were rounded up and questioned.

Amnesty International uncovered multiple cases of human rights violations—including disappearances and torture—committed by military officers acting under the Security Statute. It was a scary time, even for a thirty-one-year-old foreign journalist living in Bogotá.

I no longer cringe when I see a uniform. It's true that the soldiers look a lot younger now and less offensive now that I'm in my fifties. But more than that, the parameters for the armed forces seem to be compliance with human rights and ethics. Jamundí has shattered my belief in those parameters. It is too extreme, too surreal.

I was going to end my thoughts here with the saying, "Truth is stranger than fiction," in honor of my novelist friend. But as I think of the fear and authoritarianism of the past, I will conclude with another quotation, from George Santayana: "Those who do not remember history are condemned to repeat it."

TransMilenio III

I have a master's degree in journalism and consider myself an educated and well-traveled person. I grew up with subway systems and am an urban creature.

But I stared at the new TransMilenio bus line maps with their different colors and numbers and felt like crying. I asked at least four people how my bus route had changed and got four different answers. I wasn't the only one. The overnight change in bus schedules and color codes set the system into pandemonium.

It was more than just transitional chaos. The unplanned way in which the changes took effect broke faith with the sense that the TransMilenio belonged to everyone as a source of identity and pride. Already the cracks had begun to show. In the early days of the system five years ago, women, children, and senior citizens routinely got offered seats, up and beyond the few designated "blue" seats for these categories. Now anything goes. People don't respect the blue seats, and even robberies are frequent.

The system, I try to rationalize, is still much superior to the disorganized chaos of belching buses racing each other to pick up the most fares. The TransMilenio is still a source of civic pride, but its very success is taxing its infrastructure.

Until the overhaul in the schedule, the general consensus was that crowded cars and robberies were the price to pay for extremely fast and efficient service. Some 1.3 million riders now use the TransMilenio, with its 7 major hubs, 114 stations, and 841 buses. The fare is 1,200 pesos, or about fifty U.S. cents. The Trans-Milenio had transformed the city and created urban solidarity.

Riders learned to stand in line and wait in an orderly fashion for their buses without pushing or shoving. They learned how to use the transit cards instead of paying conductors directly, and they learned how to read relatively sophisticated signage.

However, the routing overhaul and subsequent signage change was announced only a week before, and very little attention was paid to public education. To complicate things, a new Trans-Milenio line opened up, with an expected additional 400,000 users daily. Buses were taken off old routes to serve the new ones, and there simply weren't enough buses to go around. That meant delays.

To make things even worse, passengers had become used to buying cards with multiple rides to avoid standing in line. The multiple-journey cards ran out, and people found themselves in long lines to pay for single trips. Buses that went by with "Out of Service" signs after no other bus had passed in a half hour caused protests.

On May 9, six hundred TransMilenio users took over the road at the Portal del Norte, the TransMilenio hub in the northern part of the city. Impeding access to the road, they chanted and screamed, decrying the bus delays and the scarcity of the green feeder buses known as *alimentadores*, which go off into the neighborhoods. They protested the lack of multifare cards and the general confusion caused by the overhaul of the routes and signage. The northern TransMilenio line was paralyzed for three hours by the protesters.

What had been a model of urban planning, at least initially, became a case study in a negative relationship between provider and consumer. I find myself now taking taxis instead of the TransMilenio—but few can afford my stopgap solution.

That observation points to another concern about the Trans-Milenio. When it first started, quite a few middle-class people took it to work or at least used it on the two days a week when they had *pico y placa*, mandatory nonuse of their car for environmental reasons. When the TransMilenio buses began to get overcrowded and to experience an accompanying increase in common crime, most middle-class people stopped using them. Yet, like the New York subway system, the TransMilenio has tremendous potential as a multiclass rapid-transit system. Only one of my Colombian-born middle-class friends uses it on a daily basis to cross the entire city in a half hour to her work. She lives at the end of the line.

It's more than a story of a transport system. The TransMilenio shaped *bogotanos*' way of thinking about their city, and it compelled many residents of Bogotá from elsewhere to feel identity and civic pride. It integrated the city's poorest neighborhoods with its richest ones and gave them both equal priority along the bus routes. Green feeder buses work their way among unpaved and rocky roads in sprawling poor barrios like Usme and Ciudad Bolívar. Making its infrastructure work is an important challenge.

TransMilenio is hope, and Colombians need hope. As the country stands posed between war and peace, between modernization and rampant poverty, I can only think of the challenge of the TransMilenio as a symbol of the other challenges to come.

Truth and Reparations

I've received an e-mail from an anthropologist friend about an upcoming conference at the Javeriana University. For the most part, I avoid conferences here. When I'm at Harvard, I keep in touch with Colombia through conferences and talks. Talking heads are my lifeline there.

But here I listen to taxi drivers and shopkeepers, go to dinners, and have incessant coffees; I shop and ride the buses and stroll the Séptima. The talking heads can wait until my return to Cambridge in August. Nevertheless, the title of the conference draws my attention: "Truth and Reparations in Colombia from the Victims' Perspective."

The war is not over, and people are already thinking about the kind of reconciliation issues that usually come up postconflict. Perhaps that's because war and peace throughout the country are like a checkerboard. Half the country is in conflict, and the other half is at least thinking about postconflict. My experience in Central America tells me that war doesn't miraculously end and peace begin. There's a process of truth finding, perhaps reparations or not, and then the emergence of new types of problems like juvenile delinquency and organized crime. Some in Colombia are at least beginning to think about these problems. Negotiations have begun with one of the guerrilla groups, and many members of the paramilitary have allegedly laid down their arms. Yet it's very unclear where Colombia is headed. Maybe I need some talking heads after all.

The auditorium is packed. The Jesuit university has managed to draw a crowd of students, intellectuals, gray-haired folk, and jean-clad youngsters, as well as government representatives. The audience is sprinkled with blacks with dreadlocks, well-dressed grandmothers, and indigenous people. It is hard to tell who is an interested observer and who might be a victim.

Eduardo Pizarro, head of the Colombian Commission for Reparation and Reconciliation, sits by himself. Pizarro, who has lost two brothers to the civil strife, spent years in exile, moving from one university to another in the United States and Canada as a visiting scholar. He is now a polemical figure. Many feel that he has sold out, since the commission is often seen as a government charade, with paramilitary demobilization a cosmetic measure to allow the group to retain power and economic privileges.

Iván Orozco, a professor from the Universidad de los Andes, talks about how the Colombian situation is very different from other transition processes. In the shift from dictatorships to democracies in Latin America's southern cone, for instance, victimization could be perceived as "vertical," with clear lines between the *buenos* and the *malos*—the good guys and the bad guys. In Colombia, such clear lines do not exist, he said; victimization is "horizontal," and pardon perhaps will have to be reciprocal.

My friend Angelika Rettberg is speaking. She bridges a lot of my worlds. Now a professor at the Universidad de los Andes, she was a very active member of the Colombian Colloquium in Cambridge. When she returned to Bogotá three years ago, she almost single-handedly organized the launching of the *ReVista* issue I edited on Colombia, "Beyond Armed Actors." Moreover, she is an expert on the comparative reconciliation processes in Central America. And it is in Central America that I began to think about peace, truth finding, and reconciliation.

Camila de Gamboa, a professor from the Universidad del Rosario, then begins to explain different forms of restorative justice. She's talking about how the truth is fragmented, about how a democratic society coexists with political and social exclusion, about how, in the haste to reach peace, almost anything becomes negotiable, that violence and war are seen as problems rather than as a public construct. In Colombia, she is saying, there is an identity of violence, an identity of exclusion. Reparations must be collective, and not just specific concessions by the government in power.

The word "collective" jolts my memory. My search for understanding for responsibility, peace, and reconciliation had begun many years before my wartime experience in Central America. I was in my junior year at Barnard College in New York City when riots broke out in Harlem, the black community just a few blocks away from the university. Looting and beatings swept through the adjacent neighborhood, and we all wondered if the violence would come closer. I asked my friend Frank, a soft-spoken black Catholic from a working-class family in Mississippi, if he would protect me if violence came near the university. It was sort of a rhetorical question. Frank and I studied together. We were both struggling economically in an elite university, and we both felt sort of out of place in an environment of privilege.

But Frank's answer was unexpected. He looked at me and said honestly, "No, I wouldn't."

"But aren't we friends?" I wailed.

"Yes," he answered. "But don't you believe in original sin?"

That was the sin that the white people of the United States had visited on the blacks, all of us whites, even those whose fathers and grandfathers were living on other shores during slavery. And the reparations had to be deeper than one friend, deeper than many study sessions. It was something there, silent and unsaid, dark and deep, something in which we all shared no matter how liberal or nonviolent we were.

That was an important lesson on how societies must assume the collective burden of guilt and also the responsibility for making a difference. It is as true in Colombia as in the case of race relations in the United States or in the case of today's German youth in regards to the Holocaust past. We cannot separate ourselves from our societies, no matter how invisible the wounds are, no matter how invisible the war in our daily lives.

Dreaming of Journalism II

I sink into the plush leather chairs in the waiting room of the rector's office at the National University. No traffic noise penetrates from the outside. I am swiftly offered my choice of *tinto*, the ubiquitous small cup of coffee, or *agua aromática*, herbal tea. I am waiting for the newly appointed rector, Moisés Wasserman, and for my colleague Azriel Bibliowicz.

Azriel, a professor at the university in the Department of Film and Television, shows up. His presence calms me. I've been here nine months now and have produced a sixty-page document about what a graduate program in journalism would look like.

Disturbances at the university and a hiring freeze have meant that we couldn't move forward on the project. I fear that if a director isn't hired before I leave in late August, the project will remain on paper. This meeting is a turning point: the rector's attitude will determine what happens.

We are called inside. Dr. Wasserman is a chemist, a distinguished-looking man about my age with a son who is in a post-doctoral program at Harvard. I register that fact, hoping that somehow we can maintain ties when we return. Right off, Wasserman says, "Journalism is important," and then spends a few minutes on a discussion of the difference between a journalism program and communications. Azriel and I are insistent: semiotics is not what this country needs.

But here we are in a catch-22. A hiring freeze is on, and it's impossible to hire from within, because there are simply no journalists at the country's largest public university. Maybe a few slots can be shifted from some other department so journalists can be hired as professors. Maybe. Wasserman cites the example of petroleum studies, which the university also needs. It is almost impossible to get people, even when the slots are available, because private industry pays more than the public university. That's true for oil, I'm sure, but I'm not quite sure it's true for journalism.

Wasserman is far from negative; he is down-to-earth and realistic, asking probing questions. He finally asks Azriel and me to draw up a short strategic plan. He is cordial, but I leave with a deep sense of pessimism. I think of the regional journalists who so much need their public university to provide them with a framework in which to learn. I think of the good journalists who could be better with the proper training. They shouldn't have to go to the United States or Spain or Mexico or have to extract practical nuggets from more theoretical communications programs.

The university is a high-quality public university by any standards. When I lived in Colombia the first time, the university was constantly closed because of political protests. Now the emphasis is on learning and on preparation for careers. The protests that rocked the university in November stemmed from an academic reform about which students were not consulted, reforms that some students and radical professors considered "neoliberal" because they reflected the U.S. university system. Yet the slowness and cumbersome quality of a public institution is precisely what we are experiencing with the journalism program.

My formal Fulbright assignment was to the National University, but my work is conceptual and communicative. The reason I haven't been teaching classes is precisely because no journalism faculty yet exists. The departments I have visited thus far are all fairly modern; notices of cultural events and study-abroad opportunities grace the bulletin boards.

Azriel invites me for coffee to discuss our next steps in strategic planning. We go across the spacious campus, which makes free bicycles available for between-building transport, to the Agriculture Department. Azriel says the department cafeteria has the best coffee. He is right.

On our way out, I notice that a bulletin board is dedicated to the life of Ernesto "Che" Guevara. A huge mural dedicated to Che was ordered painted over earlier in the year, and I wonder if the bulletin board is a response to this administrative decision or whether students who do their internships in Colombia's countryside become radicalized.

Azriel offers to drop me at the university entrance so I can take a bus, but as we are leaving, cars in front of it are making U-turns. "There's trouble up ahead," a driver in one of the cars calls out. "Rock throwers."

Azriel takes me to another entrance, far from the trouble. I decide to walk back to the first entrance to see what is happening. The rock-throwing students are gone; perhaps they were only a handful, enough to make some trouble. I pick up a flyer. It is a protest against the Free Trade Agreement, which Colombia is negotiating with the United States.

I walk on. On the opposite sidewalk, I see a huge green army tank and a bunch of soldiers. I cross the street. Nobody else is looking at the tank. It is merely waiting, an ominous and silent part of the scenery.

The state has managed to mobilize the soldiers quickly, I think. If only it could do that for a journalism program. Or even oil.

CAFAM

My Fulbright year in Bogotá began in a five-star hotel.

All the Fulbright fellows, mostly a group of enthusiastic U.S. students and a couple of us professors, were whisked three hours down the road to a luxurious hotel in the hot region—*tierra caliente*—of Melgar. I found the name of the hotel, Kualamaná, almost impossible to pronounce, so I ended up calling it CAFAM, the name of the hotel complex.

We didn't have much time to use the enormous swimming pool or the manicured miniature golf course, but we did manage to enjoy the lively discothèque, where seven-year-old kids hung out with their parents and white-haired *abuelitos* at 11 p.m. That was something you almost never see in the United States.

What I remember most about the hotel was the frigid air conditioning of the conference room and the intensity of the seminars. Some friends invited me back to CAFAM in Melgar for a weekend a couple of months ago. I felt disoriented. The pool wasn't as elegant as I remembered; I couldn't find the golf course, although I didn't try very hard; the dining rooms looked different. I mostly spent time reading and talking to my friends by the pool. I can't remember the name of the original hotel, only "CAFAM." I finally decided that I had been mistaken and that the Fulbright orientation had been someplace else—maybe at Colsubsidio, one of the other resorts for workers and their families. During orientation, I was perhaps still on information overload. After all, I hadn't lived in Colombia for more than twenty years.

Fast-forward to June, the month, not me. I'm sort of in exit mode, although I don't want to be—I still have more than two months before I leave Colombia. The rain in Bogotá has been incessant, and I really want to get out to *tierra caliente* to feel the heat of the sun steam out the cold that has worked its way into every bone of my body. At a Fulbright social event, I hear someone mention the orientation for Colombian students going to the United States. The orientation will be at CAFAM in Melgar. My mind immediately flashes back to the frigid conference rooms and then to the almost-empty saltwater swimming pool and the pleasant rays of the tropical sun. "Do you need a speaker?" I volunteer to a Fulbright program director.

So here I am back at CAFAM at Melgar, speaking on U.S. culture and language. The hotel is definitely the same place as my orientation. Only now I am a speaker and don't have an obligation to attend all the seminars. The quality of the students overwhelms me: there's a mom with two kids who is going to Rutgers to do her doctorate in gender studies; a recently married couple who will be going to Florida—he's a lawyer who is pursuing a doctorate in philosophy, and his wife finished her doctoral thesis for a Spanish university. There are almost fifty students, who will be pursuing dance, political science, international relations, film studies, public health, biology, public administration, finance, and other subjects in the United States. The terms of the fellowship obligate the students to return to Colombia.

I resist the temptation to spend all my time talking to the students, and head for the pool. The sun is beating down, and I plunge into the water. The pool, even though it is landscaped with exuberant tropical flowers, could be just about anywhere. So I wander. There's a sign pointing to a zoo. I decide to investigate.

It's quite a hike from the hotel, and as I wander down the road through the CAFAM complex, I see a group of people playing volleyball. It's an unusual mix: several women who look like housewives or maybe store clerks, a silver-haired man, some scrawny young folk, and a couple of tall black men who look more like basketball players. A battered bus stands in the parking lot with a sign "Universidad Nacional, Palmira," and I realize that what has brought these disparate citizens together in a friendly sports competition is their shared public university experience.

All along the side of the road are tiny bungalows, and I now remember passing them when I came with my friends. I glimpse off in the distance. There is another hotel, a four-star hotel, and that's where I stayed before.

This is indeed a complex, a multiclass vacation resort with something for everyone. I've heard of CAFAM for years, gone to the sprawling and economical supermarket in Bogotá by that name. And this is my third time here this year. But probably, like many vacationers, I am too involved with the splendid warmth of the sun and vacation or seminar routine to explore CAFAM as a social institution.

Memory is once again tugging at me. I know maids and workers who take English courses at CAFAM in Bogotá. I met an indigenous woman in Pasto who had received CAFAM's Woman of the Year prize. And I recall that CAFAM received an award from UNESCO for contributing to adult literacy.

More than life at the swimming pool at my five-star hotel, CA-FAM—which stands for Caja de Compensación Familiar (Family Benefit Fund)—is one of those Colombian dreams, just like the students taking off to pursue higher education.

Private companies contribute to the fund for their workers, a bit like Social Security in the States, but the money goes for everything from education and professional training to health care and affordable vacation resorts for working-class and middle-class Colombians.

Some 22 million people, or one out of every two Colombians, live below the poverty line, according to 2006 United Nations statistics, and the income inequality in Colombia is among the worst in Latin America.

In a nation of unequals, family benefit funds like CAFAM and Colsubsidio constitute a particularly Colombian vision of income redistribution. In theory at least, they are much closer to the European concept that people—of all social classes—have the fundamental right to health, welfare, housing, and even vacations. In Bogotá, I've seen CAFAM eyeglass shops and gone for groceries to CAFAM supermarkets; I've certainly known people who have camped with a CAFAM program or taken swimming lessons at one of its pools.

It just took a short hike from a five-star swimming pool to begin to understand the inclusiveness of the concept—and to muse on the fact that, even within inclusion, there is exclusion. The rural poor and the urban unemployed cannot and do not share in the benefits of this vision. For a minute, I'm back in Bogotá, thinking of the woman with the worn face but soft features and gently wavy hair who sits with her infant on the sidewalk outside the Ley variety store on the Séptima. I can't tell her age; she looks twenty, going on seventy, with kind, sad, intelligent eyes. I often buy a bit of bread or milk for her, and she hands me a stick of incense with a tiny Garfield calendar. Thus far it has been a silent exchange, but someday I will ask her where she is from, what her story is. There is no CAFAM for her, at least not in this gritty urban life.

Perhaps Luis Alberto Moreno, the Colombian president of the Inter-American Development Bank, was thinking of women like my street friend, in his op-ed piece in the June 8 *El Tiempo*, when he cited the 360 million Latin Americans, 70 percent of those in the region, who live on less than US$300 monthly: "This enormous mass is excluded from the most basic services, such as drinking water and sewage, without even talking about housing, education and, above all, employment." Let alone low-cost vacations and a chance at an egalitarian volleyball game.

I wonder if the existence of the CAFAM vision, the recognition of certain economic and social rights, means that it could be extended downward to the poorest of the poor, given political will and economic resources.

A soft tropical breeze blows through my hair and brings my

mind back to Melgar. I think of the fifty Fulbright students who will be an investment in Colombia's future.

I wander down to the zoo, past the playful monkeys and creepy reptiles. A large crowd is gathered. A blue-and-green peacock is spreading open its joyous plumage.

Epilogue

Manuela was only two months old when I finished my Fulbright fellowship. She's now two and a half. While her parents spend a year at Harvard's Nieman Foundation for Journalism, she's learning to say "I want a cookie" and to sing "Twinkle, Twinkle, Little Star." She shares and she negotiates in a way I associate with Colombians far older than she.

I sit with her parents in a videoconference of the Colombian Colloquium with important civil society actors in Bogotá. We discuss land reform and developing a strategy for peace.

I realize that for me there is now no "here" and "there." Colombia is a part of me, wherever I am. I also realize that in Manuela's short lifetime some things have changed in Bogotá and in Colombia—but the challenge of building democratic institutions and achieving peace remains the same.

Colonel Byron Carvajal was sentenced in May 2008 to fifty-four years in prison for masterminding the massacre at Jamundí in which ten policemen and a civilian died. The trial in a civilian court lasted one year and two months. Fourteen other soldiers were also convicted and sentenced to prison terms of more than fifty years each.

President Álvaro Uribe is once again talking about reelection, although his chances seem to be hurt by Colombians' anxiety about a pyramid scheme that is affecting their pocketbooks.

According to the Inter American Press Association, journalists continue to be threatened and are increasingly targets of libel suits to create an atmosphere of self-censorship. They have also been subjects of accusations by President Uribe, who branded some reporters as "permissive accomplices of terrorism."

After eight years of operation, the TransMilenio has a 76 percent approval rate, but now the government is talking about building a controversial subway system, as well as extending TransMilenio lines.

People still flock to the *ciclovía* every Sunday, and theatre, film, and song festivals have multiplied.

The newspaper *El Espectador* has returned to its old roots of operating as a daily newspaper, giving Colombians more venues for obtaining information. The National University has begun to consider establishing a journalism track within its political science department.

Many paramilitary forces have demobilized, but some are said to operate outside the law in common crime. Others have made a successful transition to civilian life.

Colombians wait to see what U.S. president Barack Obama will bring in terms of foreign policy, in particular his stance on how to handle the drug trade.

Colombians wait to see whether Álvaro Uribe will run again for president and, if not, who the candidates will be.

The statistics change, and yet the big picture remains the same. I can only hope that Manuela can return to a Bogotá with a continuing atmosphere of civic responsibility and to a country on its way to peace.